CW00957201

The Bedside Urban Voltaire

The Bedside Urban Voltaire

Jack McLean

To Simon Leslie-Carter
stephen

Jack McLean

LOCHAR PUBLISHING · MOFFAT · SCOTLAND

To those who have ever taken a drink in a public house, and to those who have supplied it. But most of all to Harry Reid.

© Jack McLean 1990
Published by Lochar Publishing Limited
    MOFFAT DG10 9JU

British Library Cataloguing in Publication Data
McLean, Jack
    The bedside urban voltaire
    I. Title
    828.91407

ISBN 0–948403–21–7

Typeset in 11pt on 13pt New Century Schoolbook by
Dumfries ITeC
and printed in Great Britain by BPCC Wheaton's Ltd,
Exeter.

Contents

Foreword

Nothing in the *Glasgow Herald* has given me more trouble than the Jack McLean column. Yet I would not be without it. Indeed, it is my belief that long after we are gone people will be reading Jack McLean not as a prophet but as a chronicler of his age.

When people write in complaint about Jack's columns, I tell them that he is a satirist who uses the rhetoric of vituperation in order to achieve comic effects and deflate the pomposites and hypocrisies of the day. But I am also conscious that it is hard for people who have been the objects of his derision to take so Olympian a view. People have been grievously offended by Jack's column, people who themselves are engaged in the hurly-burly of journalism. Jack himself, however, is genuinely surprised when people take his remarks ill. His intention is to ridicule, to send up. He hurts but he is not malicious.

As a writer Jack is original. He went to no school of journalism. Indeed, he was educated at Edinburgh School of Art and then became a teacher. My impression is that his time at the chalkface was not happy. Jack is not a natural pedagogue, I would guess, and it must have come as a relief to himself and his employers that his translation into journalism slowly grew to the point where he could give up the teaching.

He was discovered when Harry Reid and I were colleagues on the *Scotsman*. We ran his 2000-word essays in the weekend section there, and they were received with some pleasure in Glasgow. When I became editor of the *Herald* nine years ago, and invited Jack to become one of our columnists, his work had a very different impact. When in the *Scotsman* it had been like a sermon on a distant hill. Now Jack had entered the drawing rooms of the Glasgow bourgeoisie. Their first reaction was of shock it was as if a drunk had staggered in through the french windows and had been sick on the carpet.

Slowly the shock wore off and Jack began to be accepted. He has written no more moving column than his tribute to his mother after her death. From that piece I date his acceptance by the family of *Herald* readers. Not that he will ever be their unanimous favourite. You either love the Urban Voltaire or you hate him. There seems to be no middle ground. You have to hand it to Jack: he dishes it out but he takes it too, for no *Herald* writer has been more publicly reviled in our letters column.

Once when I was a member of the judging panel for the Scottish press awards, Jack was in contention for the award of columnist of the year. For obvious reasons I fell out of the judging. The rest of the panel was split between those who voted for him enthusiastically and those who would allow him to win only over their dead bodies. So immovable were the opposing camps that the chairman had to break the deadlock with his casting vote.

Jack's political progress has been typical of the age. Of impeccable working-class credentials he has moved progressively away from the Labour politics he inherited. He has slowly become a member of the bourgeoisie. He now even owns a flat, for goodness sake. He has drifted to the right. Some of his views seem to me to be positively conservative.

Yet he is uneasy with his bourgeois fate. His life style may have changed but his class loyalty remains strong. He has evoked very vividly his own progression through the shifting strata of Thatcher's Britain and Lally's Glasgow. What gives his work its merit is his clear eye, his refusal to be impressed by convention and authority, his honesty about himself and his disrespect for mere politeness. He has the capacity to voice what many people often think but rarely dare say. He has the courage to be wrong.

From time to time the metropolitan newspapers express interest in Jack as a quick fix for their blandness. So far Jack has resisted the lure. He knows, I think, that Glasgow is his patch and that he would find it hard going in more anonymous and luxuriant metropolitan pastures. He is of his place and his time, but the hypocrisies and pretensions which he pricks are in eternal need of deflation.

As editors we face problems with Jack's copy. Sometimes he pushes the limits. Sometimes we excise passages that will try the readers' patience too far. There is after all no victory in making someone turn the page in a spirit of rejection. Sometimes, we think, Jack puts in things for us to take out. Yet there is a limit for us too. We cannot take too much out or else we will destroy the very qualities that make Jack's writing what it is — the keen eye, the descriptive prose, the cadences of demotic speech which he so faithfully expresses. Jack does not invent the forceful language of the street but his prose is redolent of it, together with a more ornate quality which I can only describe as Edwardian.

Finally, let me set the record straight about the title of Urban Voltaire which has been attached to Jack. Some people thought that Jack himself vaingloriously adopted it. The truth is that Harry Reid and I invented the name in our *Scotsman* days and it has stuck. It was inspired by the Thurber short story about the Rustic Voltaire, a man who sat on a cracker barrel in a country store and had the answers to everything. Jack's omniscience is sometimes breathtaking but it is blessed by a sense of the ridiculous, not least about himself. I am delighted that Lochar has decided to publish a collection of his columns: they read as commentary on the age, and will be enjoyed for many years to come.

ARNOLD KEMP
Editor of the *Glasgow Herald*

Clothes Maketh the Man?

Big Girls in Ankle Socks

WHO THINKS UP jokes? Who is it that sits in reverie in some dark corner and thinks them up? Don't tell me all that sociological blah about them being developments of old folk traditions, even subliminal ones. That might be socio, but it surely isn't logical. For a start, somebody, back in the beginning and huddling in caves, thought up the folk tradition. There are other things like that, which seem utterly inexplicable. I suppose football chants is one. Clothes are another.

There are always lots of opinions about the style of clothes, and many an explanation is made by the most absurd academics. The latter have often expounded the thesis that in times of plenty – say the 'Sixties – clothes were skimpy, and the microskirt comes instantly to mind, and in times of hardship such as the days of the New Look and Austerity or in our own stirring era, garments become positively voluminous. There are simply too many contradictions in this argument to bother with it. I only have a thousand words in the drivel. In short, there seems no rhyme nor reason to clothes wearing at all, at least as far as fashions in it goes. Think of socks.

Socks came to my attention some time back. As I sit each day after four in a South-Side hostelry sipping soda water and lime, I watch the merry brats of the august Shawlands Academy go skipping up the road, happy with their successes of the day and keen to re-enact their achievements in front of their luckless parents. In the last few months, as I gazed sadly through the window, I have seen the female of the brat species, and noted a singular phenomenon. The bratettes are into socks.

Oh it is not simple socks. It is ankle socks. A strange thing this. I am sure that it is undeniably true that this

11

trend in young female attire is very welcome, especially to hard-pressed, hard-up mums for whom the weekly expenditure on tights once probably exceeded their rates bill. It is doubtless more healthy as well. Certainly ankle socks look smart and fresh on young girls feet. And on big girls they even look, to salacious chaps like your Urban V here, rather sexy. The latest big girl to shove her plates into ankle socks was none other than Lady Di herself and very tasty it was too.

An editor told me that the mode was probably started by our fashion-conscious Princess of Wales, but I think not. (In fact, as I remember it, the wearing of ankle socks by any grown woman, especially her man's socks, was, when teamed up with a pair of stained fluffy bedroom slippers and a head tied in a turban, a sure sign of a Glasgow hairy). It seems to me that the young Mrs. Windsor has another, deeper reason for going about clad in what, in my day, was a positive badge of childhood for lassies, as much a badge as short trousers were for lads. This brings about another enquiry.

Why are the girls choosing to wear wee daft socks? When I was a teenager every lassie I knew was wetting herself to get allowed to wear stockings and grow up. You got used to the terribly wee spindly legs draped with ugly nylon folds. The average schoolgirl looked like a washing on two poles. As for we chaps, I still remember the name of the last boy in the class who got himself into long trousers. It was Coutts. (I'll bet THAT embarrasses him even yet; certainly now that I have revealed it to the world).

Dear God, the desire to grow up, to be a man, my son, was overwhelming, and the Earth was going to be yours and everything that's in it. I know Kipling meant much by the words I have just paraphrased. My pals and me, we translated his noble sentiments into an awesome hungering for a pair of drainpipe trousers and a white shortie raincoat.

With a bright scarlet lining. It was no good without the red lining.

There were thousands of little icons on the road to adulthood like shortie coats though; strange nuance-shrouded touchstones of manhood quite impenetrable by any parent. I still recollect my mum's opacous bemusement when I point-blank refused to accept the compromise of a pair of semi-pointed shoes. How could I explain it: that such a half way house showed up your childhood to your peers as no ordinary pair of school shoes ever could.

It was a silly time and a silly age. For successive generations of teenagers it has continued too. I remember the tight arcana of my teenhood apparel. The shirt collar turned up, the short bumfreezer jacket, the drainies, the buckled shoes, slim jim ties, hair quoiffed with Tru-Gel. You think I looked daft? You should have seen the girls. They wore sticky-out dresses with petticoats starched enough to cut their calves to the bone. Their hair was so french-combed and lacquered that steel combs used to snap in it. Their stilletto heels defied gravity. The littlest girls used to look like pin cushions the wrong way up. They wore lipstick of so pale a hue that their coupons looked somehow like a negative photo. Their teeth were darker than their lips for heaven's sake. Teenagers have looked worse though, in the past twenty five years. But always behind it all was a longing to be older, to be older than a mere child. Boys couldn't wait to cover up their legs with flannel, and girls saw nylons as the first and fundamental desideratum in the path to adulthood. Could this phenomenon, this wearing of ankle socks, could this signify a change in what was once an ever-hastening of adulthood, the shortening of childhood. Could it be that the girls don't especially WANT to grow up too quickly, or even at all?

When I was a child, I spake as a child, I understood as a child, I thought as a child: but when I became a man, I put away childish things. Perhaps the kids know it. They might

13

have to see through a glass darkly, as my generation doubtless did too early, but not now the kids may be saying, but later. And the question is: who started THAT?

Give a Man a Uniform

I'VE ALWAYS fancied myself in uniform. I mean military uniform of course and not a pip below the rank of major at that. I would want something snappy perhaps with riding breeches and boots which practically glow in the dark, Cherry Blossomed by an especially obsequious batman. 'I say Higgins,' I'd drawl nonchalantly, 'spit and polish on the old Sam Browne will yer? There's a good chap!' I'd say. 'Decent sort of feller,' I'd affirm to the junior officers in the mess.

I probably got this desire from the Da. He'd been a regular before the War and was wont to recount dull tales of service overseas in Shanghai and Cairo and such far-off places. He once told me how he and his fellow squaddies would get uniforms run up by local coolie tailors for a pittance. The result was that the private soldier serving in the China of the 'Twenties possessed a dress uniform so elaborate and fanciful that even a particularly dandiacal Ruritanian prince would have felt half naked. Eventually the C.O. put a stop to it all when he discovered that every man on the parade ground looked like a Field bloody Marshall.

The Da continued in uniform: he was a school janitor. He took this uniform to ridiculous lengths too. He insisted on a white shirt with a starched collar instead of the regulation blue shirt and his cap badge was burnished enough to act as a heliograph for the other side of the City. He would have been the only school janitor in the world who'd have worn spurs for God's sake if he could have got away with it. Truth to tell my Da absolutely loathed uniform, but his notion in all the things was that if you had to do it you might as well overdo it. So he did.

Clothes Maketh the Man?

Most uniforms look rather splendid though. Almost all females can turn a uniform, no matter how silly, into apparel bursting with lust at the seams. I cite schoolgirls, policewomen, and air hostesses as examples. I am bound to state that the above is nothing but sexism though you can look no further than your local bank in which you will find all the ladies in sweaters with the company logo or wee overalls with the bank's name prominently displayed on the right ti... breast, while the chaps, being considered more august by virtue of their gender, are cutting about in their own grey suits. Doubtless there is a reason for this. I think it is probably to do with making the bints subservient.

I suppose part of the reason for uniform of any kind is exactly the subservience notion. What's wrong with that anyway? I WANT railwaymen to be subservient, and police people too. Well, if not subservient, at least polite instead of arrogant and insulting. I will tell you this though. If you are wanting such employees of ours as the above to talk to you like a human being you will have to ensure that the gear you stick them into is going to lend dignity to them. As I think I may have intimated the other week to you division out there it is my opinion that the ridiculous BR uniforms look dafter than anything Coco ever wore and the reason for all rail people's surliness is that they feel a laughing stock for their entire working life. The polis are a different matter altogether. The polis should not be persuaded, and we should not permit this to occur, into over-smart uniforms. Stick a poli into dark glasses, a black leather jerkin, an American-style dark blue shirt covered in lurid flashes and badges, shove that on his back and you will be getting a fascist carried away with himself. If our police are going to continue to be wonderful (Ha!) then insist upon the dreary old blue serge and the flat-feet boots. That good old image of the cheery bobby on the beat might just be an image but I am not frightened by the sight of our polis the way I am by the magnificent militaria enjoyed by the polizei on the continent. Polis and railwaymen and G.P.O. people and bus drivers and all those public employees clad in uniform are to be joined by another group, you may have read the other day. Glasgow Corporation decided to put their staff in the Housing Department into a nice, bright, jangly, new outfit. Instead of the surly, boring, shabby old staff you encounter in the department, you will soon be greeted by surly, boring, anything but shabby personnel clad in bright red sweaters and smart blouses, and red ties and scarves. I want them in bright red suspender belts myself, but only for the girls. I simply don't care what colour the men's pants are.

A particularly daft Conservative councillor has of course complained about the choice of bright red for the uniform. He says the Labour group chose the colour because of their political ideology. I reason if that were the case they'd have chosen a pale pink with a wee stripe of yellow denoting corrupti... business consultancy. The daft Conservative councillor can surely find more than the bloody colour to object about in this daft and expensive scheme to develop what a 'housing official' described as 'a process in improving customer service' of which the introduction of uniform was 'an important psychological step'.

Myself, I do not want Glasgow Corporation to indulge in any psychological steps at all. I want them to indulge in cost-cutting steps when it comes to improving customer service so that more customers can get some of it. Glasgow Corporation and, indeed, the Strathclyde gauleiters are too damned keen these days in promoting their image anyway. I am sick of seeing eighty brand new types of bus every week and new logos stamped across them every second day. I am fed up with glossy little pamphlets telling me the education service is going from strength to strength when I know full well it is falling apart. I do not want my cleansing operative nicking about in an outfit designed by Yves Saint Laurent: I want a dustbin man. Let the good gauleiters wear uniform. May I suggest a number in red and yellow with a cap with bells on it. It'd suit them to perfection.

Eat Your Blazer

IT WAS Mr. Grimwig, you may remember, who maintained that if that young wimp Oliver Twist was found to be honest he would eat his head. Many a time another chap had been heard to offer to eat his hat. A splendid variation on this Pickwickian suggestion was reported at the weekend when Mr. Frank Docherty, a well-known dominie, (and renowned as 'Handsome Frank'), rose to his feet at last weekend's MARXISM TODAY festival and declared that he 'would eat his blazer.' Most revealing.

For a start, Mr. Docherty, dominie, WAS wearing a blazer. Come to that, so was I. But there were hordes of blazers about. Strangely a goodly number of the chaps sporting this hangover from Britain's nautical past were, I noticed, teachers. In all seriousness I have to ask you lot out there if it is possible that more teachers today wear blazers than do weans? In Glasgow at any rate. In the culture city it seems that the only schools which oblige their brats to don the traditional raiment are the toffee-nosed institutions with the bought house parents. It is, of course, the height of daftness to find the better-off parents putting their children into blazers which last two years while the poorer mums and dads stick expensive leather bombers which last six months on their weans backs. But not surprising. What IS surprising is that the blazer seems to be back for the dads at least.

Up until I left school I never had any other kind of jacket. The primary school I went to didn't have such an affectation to a school uniform but the secondary one did. It had every affectation to a school uniform as you could imagine. Some of the better-off kids possessed a uniform elaborate enough for the Household Cavalry, for heaven's sake. The first school blazer I had was a glory to me all the same: from Paisley's it was. All right, maybe it wasn't quite Forsyth's, but it wasn't Granite House either. There was a badge sewn right into the pocket, not sewed on, but part of the blazer itself. The pride of it all.

Well, as is the way of things, pride comes before a fall and it wasn't long before my school blazer degenerated just as my academic career did. By the time I was being exhorted to leave the establishment to inflict myself upon an employer, my school blazer was somewhat of a hated object and was considerably less grand than the one my proud pater had shoved on me at the start of my first year. By then my academic endeavours were exiguous, to say the least, and the blazer was of cheaper import and was two years old. The only thing which held the thin fabric together was dirt, ink stains, and fag smoke. It was a far cry indeed from the expectations of the first blazer, bought two sizes too big and designed in every way to express hope for the future. My last blazer heralded failure, defeat, and parental despair.

But sure, most of you out there remember the school blazer. The faith with which you invested it when you went up to the adventure of the big school. Later you were doubtless to resent its identifying powers. I can still remember standing in my first illicit public house with my shortie raincoat buttoned fast and me sweating partly through the summer heat and partly through the excitement hoping that nobody could get a peep of the blue serge underneath. By the time I was in the business of trying to put away childish things I was celebrating the last part of the biblical quotation and looking through a glass darkly when I could find a publican daft or venal enough to serve me. Thus it was that the very notion of a blazer in adult life filled me with a feeling close to contempt. For if it wasn't wee bits of boys donning the thing it was rather ridiculous adults. Bogus majors or Squadron leaders wore them, with non-entitled regimental ties. The eternal emblem of the bounder, as ineluctable to the species as a handlebar moustache. They weren't the worst of the blazerites either. There were the old bowling club johnnies with silly badges on the pocket and weighed down by metal tokens on the lapels denoting their frequent captaincies. And if you thought they were bad, there was still the Jordanhill PE students who had a breast pocket badge on their blazers exotically complex enough as to be in direct contradiction to their simple minds. To the above, a blazer was for strutting in, with a hint of stupidity to go with it.

It was, you can understand then, years before I brought myself to purchasing a blazer. I've had several since, all dark blue, double breasted. There is nothing as smart as such a piece of finery. Teamed with the ubiquitous grey flannels and the white shirt you cannot go wrong. I affect the black and silver tie of Magdalen College, Oxford to go with the ensemble (I'll bet you didn't know I was at Magdalen College: I read Country and Western Music there). The shirt has to have double cuffs.

Strangely, such an outfit now has bourgeois connotations, as if the plain blue grey and white of the costume was somehow missuit to lofty left-wing thinking. Strangely because it is entirely descended from the day dress of the great Beau Brummell and was designed, as Max Beerbohm once pointed out, to clothe democracy, so simple was it in its demands. But it is probably changed days now, for the blazer is back and a good thing too, though I would advise Mr Frank Docherty to think again about eating his. The buttons would choke in his throat.

Kiltie Kiltie Cauld Bum

'I NOTE,' I said to the chaps in my little South-side club the other day, 'that there is some discussion this weather about the feilidh-Mor, or as it sometimes known, the breacan an fheilidh, though to be more pedantic' – at this a soft moan emanated from Leo the Tim in the corner of the bar, '– to be more exact we are talking of the philibeg'. One of the bolder denizens at this point dared to imply that he didn't have a bloody clue what we were talking about at all. I smote him smartly with my cromach. 'It seems', I continued, 'that the philibeg, to wit the kilt of our National Dress, has been somewhat in the news'.

And in the news it has. A recent lady correspondent to this blatt recently pointed out that male exclusivity of the kilt could well be at risk. She and we are not overly perturbed at the photographs of little Miss Kerry Anne McGreechan dressed up as a pipe major at the Balloch Highland games the other week. Small girls have invariably worn male highland dress when taking part in dancing competitions at such jamborees. Truth to tell I have ever experienced a certain, ahem, EMOTION at the sight of big girls in kilts as well, depending upon the length of the garment in question. But we will not go into my little interests in life this day. I would certainly deplore the regular adoption of the most marvellous national costume in the world by ladies. I include most Englishmen in this category. I will allow a chap of that nationality the wearing of the kilt in circumstances which allow for whisky and General Practice.

There is of course a reason – and a bloody good one it is too – why the English are to be forbidden the kilt. It was them, the blaggards, who stopped it for us upon pain of death or transportation. Here is what they said then.

'From and after the First Day of August 1747 no Man or Boy, within that part of Great Britain called Scotland, other than such as shall be employed as Officers or Soldiers in His Majesty's Forces, shall, on any pretence whatsoever wear or put on the clothes commonly called Highland clothes, (that is to say the Plaid, Philibeg or Little Kilt,

Clothes Maketh the Man?

Trowse, Shoulder Belts or any part whatsoever of what peculiarly belongs to the Highland Garb; and that no Tartan or partly coloured Plait or Stuff shall be used for Great Coats ...'. It was pretty comprehensive. And the Act lasted for another 35 years until the Duke of Montrose got it repealed. Forty years later George the Fourth was cavorting about Edinburgh dressed like a bigger idjit than either of the Alexander Brothers and twice as Scotch-looking.

To this day the Royals are great ones for showing off their shilpit wee knees in kilts. As far as I can see the only Royal who has legs fit for a kilt at all is the new Duchess of York, and she has a pair of pins, not to mention physique, somewhat reminiscent of the bloke on the front of Scotts Porridge Oats packets. Poor old King George looked as though his legs were pinned on to the hem. Successive official photographs of the Royal Family at Balmoral has them standing uneasily in Highland Dress, as though they were having terrible trouble with midges around the region of the groin. Perhaps they were.

One fellow who seems to have no difficulty concerning this delicate area, I mean matter, is a certain Viscount Gough. He is the fellow who was snapped by press photos at the Shetland visit of the Prince and Princess of Wales, (the Royal people just keep on cropping up this week), and had Princess Di giggling like a schoolgirl. The bold Viscount had managed to reveal unwittingly what silly Englishmen, not to mention silly schoolgirls, have always been at the most dreadful pains to know – What Scotsmen Wear Under The Kilt. As befits a decent kilt-wearer he was clad in what is often known as full Highland Dress and most imposing it probably was too. I cannot understand the reaction of photos: I should have thought most of them had seen similar phenomena before. Come to think of it, surely the good Princess has too.

It is quite astonishing how many chaps and chapettes are grimly determined to get themselves into a Scottish skirt though. Yehudi Menhuhin, of the famous Menhuhin clan, (mind you, my Da, who came from Mull, claimed that the McLean's were ever the lost tribe of Israel, and very lost indeed they must have been at that); your man Yehudi was spied in a kilt at the fiddling open of the Commonwealth fiasco. I am trying hard to think of any contemporary figure weirder than that to shove into the tartan and so far I can only come up with Alasdair Gray and I can hardly imagine him in underpants let alone a kilt.

Ach, sure there's more bizarre than that and it's me that knows it. Was it not your Urban Voltaire here who was never out of the philibeg of a Sunday morning and just before his catechism? A stirring sight he was in the fat legs. Girls used to pull my skirt up, and the coevals amongst the boys called you Kiltie Kiltie Cauld Bum. It was years later that I wore the kilt, for an expensive Edinburgh wedding. I looked like Daphne Broon.

I made my mind up upon my musings in my little South-Side club. 'Boys,' I said, 'I shall be wearing the kilt in future. The sporran. The daft jaicket with the squerr silver buttons. Breid knife down the sock. Why should the girls', I said, 'have all the best gear?'

A White Tuxedo!

WHEN YOU are a little lad you are full of ambition. Some want to be train drivers when they grow up. I never wanted to be a train driver when I grew up. I still don't. Others want to be soldiers, sailors, captains of industry. There are blokes who want to be very strange things indeed. I have a pal called Roddy who wants to be an Assistant Head Master when he grows up. (I don't blame him there – have you seen the wages?). But my ambitions were not of that order when I was a boy. My hopes were of a more, somehow spiritual, or at least aesthetic, nature. I wanted to have a thin moustache when I reached Man's Estate. And I wanted to wear, even at breakfast – ESPECIALLY at breakfast – a white tuxedo.

A dinner suit at breakfast. The very man that is. While the schmucks of this world are rattling down the muesli and berating their weans to get to school on time and screwing up the courage to kiss their now hideous bourgeois wives full on the lips, never mind with their mouths open, while these poor fools were going through such morning rituals your Urban Voltaire would be sauntering in – suavely, sophisticatedly – clad in the full evening rig and asking for a cup of Java, followed by eggs Benedict and a glass of Black Velvet. Consumed in the bath of course. That is the very start to a morning for your man here, I can tell you. But the dinner suit is the first essential.

The most essential thing about a dinner suit is of course that it is your own. I have gone through the hired dinner suit. It is a joke. The jacket always looks like it could fit Buster Crabbe. The trousers, well it was clear that Buster had swum in them, or maybe even worse. The crutch came so low that you used to trip over it during the foxtrot with a hapless bridesmaid. You wore all this at weddings.

That is another thing. A dinner suit must be worn, if it is to be worn with any panache at all, by the sort of person who is seen in it for festivals other than weddings. And, as I say, it must be your own. There is little worse than a tuxedo which doesn't fit. Unless it is a made-up bow tie. The tux must not only fit, but must show off the manly figure, or disguise the lack of one. It is the ultimate test of a tailor, a dinner jacket is. It was none other than my own tailor, the ubiquitous Ralphie Slater, who poured my physique into a tuxedo. For I – and I can reveal this to all my comrades on the Left – own a dinner jacket. White it is. I have reached my childhood ambition and now represent my brand of Socialism – the Champagne variety of course – in rare style.

I swear this is true: I look a dream in the white tux. The black evening strides display the graceful pins perfectly. The dress shirt is pristine, the brogans gleam enough to satisfy a National Service NCO. My (tied) bow tie has a jaunty spring in its step and the cummerbund, (I know – when the bloke in Henry Burton's suggested one I thought it sounded like a sex-aid too); the cummerbund hides the faint roll of burgeoning waist. I look great in the tux. If I could only get somebody else's face pasted in at the top I would pass for Don Ameche on a good night.

I have sported this implausible outfit at many an occasion. I have done Rugby Club dinners in it. I have spoken to groups of Catholics in it. I have showed off to Proddies too. I even exhibited the white tux at the last British Awards jamboree. An English erk called Desmond Wilkins, or something like it – I can't remember his exact name but I know he's married to that Esther Rantzen – wrote about that particular do. He said HE was wearing a white dinner jacket. He said he was the only one wearing a white dinner jacket. He said it was embarrassing being the only one wearing a white dinner jacket. I hope he was a lot more embarrassed when people told him he was either blind or a bloody liar. Because I wore a white DJ. I won a prize too. The ridiculous Desmond, naturally, didn't. Ha!

There is a distinct wee difficulty however in owning such a splendid outfit: you cannot wear it all the time. In fact, there are very few occasions indeed when I get the chance to star in it at all. Who knows? There might even come a time when I don't win anything at all in the British Press Awards thing and where'll I be then? It'll be cavorting about Heraghty's looking like a bloody bingo caller, won't it? The sad decline in formality within Society has put paid to dressing for dinner. All those years yearning for a dinner jacket and I now find that half the bloody population think dinner is eating crisps in front of a TV set while clad in tracksuit bottoms. It is hardly fair. It is not even British. We got this appalling casualness from the U.S. of A.

But do you know now what I am about to tell you: it came as a shock to me. It seems that the Yanks have re-discovered formality. And with it the Tux. It turns out the Yank Yuppies are practically going to bed in tuxedos. Stranger yet, the Yanks are at this moment actually celebrating the very invention of the dinner jacket. They say they discovered it exactly a hundred years ago on this day, October 10, 1886, and it was first revealed in the Tuxedo Club just thirty miles outside of New York. I have no information as to who first invented the very colour of the tuxedo and made of it the classiest garment in the history of mankind. The white DJ is a stoatir and I am all for it.

I am now almost grown up and I have reached two childhood ambitions. I have got a thin moustache and I have got a white tuxedo. There was a third ambition. The third concerned Maureen O'Hara. Sadly Miss O'Hara is a little old for what I had in mind. And so am I.

Food and Drink

Unsociable Hours

THE LICENSING LAWS in that England place,' I was saying
but the other day to Mr. Strange, well known as the
cheekiest barman in Western Europe, 'are a joke. Allow me
to illustrate,' I said, 'with a wee story about the very
birthplace of England's Bard'. So I told Mr. Strange about
Stratford-on-Avon, as I ordered a small refreshment in my
usual lordly way.

It was in Stratford-on-Avon that I truly encountered the
very daftness of that country's barbaric licensing laws. Two
very pretty young French maids came into ye olde worlde
hostelry where I was finishing off my glass just as the half
past two bell went off. It was a hot day and dusty. The little
mademoiselles asked for two petit bieres. They were
rewarded with a withering retort that the pub was now
shutting. The bemused young ladies were further told that
the pub would not be open again till 7 o'clock. They were
then informed that this would be so for every pub in the
length and breadth of the country. Your Urban Voltaire had
to intervene at that of course and tell the delightful jeunne
filles, (oh the French is getting better all the way here), that
they could drink beer till they went into a positive coma all
day in Glasgow and beyond in our fair country. I said it
almost bursting with pride while shooting malevolent looks
at the host of the hostelry. But you know, I exaggerated a
little. In fact I exaggerated very considerably indeed.

For in Glasgow this is by no means true. For some
inexplicable reason the pubs in Glasgow are open for
shorter hours than almost anywhere else in Scotland. Very
few pubs are open for business after eleven o'clock in the
real capital of Scotland and the very city which claims to
receive more tourists a year now than the Other Place. That
is not the worst of it my buckos. Think of Saturday and
Sunday, especially Sunday.

26

Sunday is the key to Saturday here. During the recent Mayfest jamboree in this city the pubs and restaurants were permitted by our wonderfully paternalistic magistrata to open till two, even three, in the morning, and I availed myself of this opportunity as I went my rounds of inspection upon all the aesthetic activity. But on Saturday it stopped at twelve or even earlier. This was because after midnight revelry itself turned into a pumpkin and horses of Fun became the rats of Sabbatarianism. For after twelve, Saturday becomes Sunday and foul merriments must cease. This is the law of the Sabbath.

Now it makes no matter if you have your Sabbath, as do Jews and Moslems, on the Saturday. It makes no difference whatsoever if you do not wish to observe any Sabbath at all not even for ten minutes let alone twenty-four miserable wee hours. A mere handful of religious maniacs insist that everybody falls into line with their superstitious ways. It seems very clear to me and damn near everybody else in this country and beyond, that daft Sabbath worshippers, (for sadly many a Christian worships Sunday rather than Christ) are perfectly entitled to their views and that neither I nor anybody else is going to drag them screaming into some dark boozer, tie them to chairs with light flex, and inject the buggers with wood alcohol. A Sabbatarian can have his Sabbath any way he wants for all I care. But – and I am sure you will follow my logic here – it don't, my dears, seem reasonable at all for this same handful of loops to close everything down against everybody else's wishes.

As you chaps out there well know, not everything IS closed down on a Sunday. The shops and markets all over Scotland are hoaching with customers determined to spend lots of dosh. But pubs? Restaurants? Why the 'authorities' appear to allow Mr. Mammon to go working throughout Sunday with the exception of permitting all-day or late opening where a glass of beer is concerned seems somewhat irrational. Why they listen at all to the mean-spirited Sunday Protestants is beyond sense.

27

The Bedside Urban Voltaire

Last Sunday, in the company of two hungry ladies, I went looking for a pub that was open which would supply us with grub. As it happens we couldn't discover a pub or restaurant capable of assuaging the pangs of hunger. This in that very city which boasts of its attraction for tourists. Eventually, after much searching we did find a splendid little bistro in the Candleriggs called 'Samovar', and I recommend their lasagna al forno no bother. It was unlicensed of course because Jesus Christ probably disapproved of a glass of red with his lasagna on a Sunday, though the pleasant waitress told us that we could have brought a drop in ourselves. It is all a great nonsense.

But even within the licensing laws there are what I think of as abuses of it. In a certain pub in Shawlands, about which I have written twice before, I witnessed an incident in which three middle aged men were refused service. This was because, they were told by the younger bartender, they were 'too casually dressed'. In the middle of a heatwave they wore open-neck shirts and light summer slacks. So did I. So did the five other toppers in the bar. But the three men were middle aged and they were, though certainly respectable, undeniably working class in speech and appearance. They are NOT the sort, it seems, to be allowed a pint on a hot day in the Granary Bar on Glasgow's south-side.

The Granary is owned by Ind Coope, but it was started up by one Ken McCulloch, native of this city. Mr McCulloch has a hand in lots of fashionable boozers. I am told that every one of them pursues this disgraceful policy of exclusion for the Untouchable castes. Perhaps I am wrong in this, in which case Mr. McCulloch, or even Ind Coope, might explain the behaviour of their employees.

The good gauleiters of Glasgow can boast all they like about the number of visitors to this city, but they will not be back if they continue to be given such churlish treatment, or are subjected to ludicrous and limiting laws set up by the whim of Sabbatarians. That's what I told the cheekiest

28

barman in Western Europe anyway as he took the glass from my hand and ushered me out the door.

The Lost Chip Shop

WHEN I WAS a kid living in the Townhead district of Glasgow, my brother and myself used to go to a cinema on the South Side. We usually preferred The Elephant because it was the grandest on the bus route, with huge hand-tinted photographs of Alan Ladd and Ava Gardner framed in improbable gilt plasterwork on the foyer walls. And when an usherette eventually discovered us halfway through the second sitting of the B Western and pitched us out into the street, it was always an incredible shock to find that it was dark outside, the street lights illuminating a steady drizzle, and giving a homely, city effect in the bright reflections of the shopfronts.

It'd be about 5.30 and we would already be late and in for trouble when we got home but it was nice coming out of the flicks into the evening rain, with people hurrying homewards, their breath propelling out of their nostrils like St George's dragon in the book illustrations, and wee women doing the shopping on the way, stuffing cauliflowers into bucket bags.

My brother and I would walk down to a particular chip shop and buy a fourpenny bag of chips which we'd share while we waited for the 104 bus to take us back to Townhead. We always went to this chip shop as their chips were the best we knew – dry and golden, crisp on the outside and powdery on the inside.

But what I really liked about the shop was the inside of it. It had rows of wooden cubicles, rather like the bars you saw in gangster films. That was where you sat if you bought a fish tea. A fish tea consisted of a large plate of fish and chips, a mug of wonderfully stewed tea, and several slices of margarined co-op Gold Medal bread. You 'sat in' for this; a quaint phrase, as though you were Charlie Parker at a gig.

There were people who ate there every night, because the food was cheap, plentiful and good. In the Depression, I'm told, the chip shop provided an inexpensive, tasty meal, and even a bit of a night out. It might puff you up unnaturally, and make you old and fat before your time, but it kept you alive.

This shop had been there a long time, and it had always been run by Enrico and his wife, a stout little woman with thick grey hair, and Mediterranean eyes as brilliant as drops of black coffee. Despite the fact that they had been in Britain for perhaps 20 or so years, they spoke English only haltingly, but they were always courteous and friendly, and everybody liked them.

It wasn't though, just the people who ran the shop which made this our usual port of call, nor the wonderful smell of cooking oil and vinegar. It was the big fish-frying machine itself. It lay against the wall opposite the counter like a great Wurlitzer organ, like an enormous ark of covenant in a wealthy synagogue. Made of chrome and opalescent glass, it was polished until it gleamed.

Both Enrico and his wife were very small and so they had made a wooden step on which they stood as they shifted the chips around in the vats of oil. That even added to the ritualistic, almost sacramental, appearance of the great machine. They looked like two high priests at an altar, swinging the monstrance. And the question which they always asked, as they piled your chips into the newspaper, sounded vaguely religious as well. 'saul anna vinegar?' they would inquire, in the same tone of voice as a priest saying mass might use.

But in the middle of this great ark, right across the length of it, was a huge panorama of a painting, protected by a curving sheet of Perspex. It was a picture of some beauty spot in Enrico's native Naples. The painting was rather inexpertly done, but it had a freshness for all that – rather like the work of Raoul Duffy.

The scene looked out across the Bay of Naples from the vantage point of a quiet, white-washed loggia. There were cypress and olive trees. The sky was a light blue and, from the way that the red roofs reflected the sun, I always imagined that it was about ten o'clock in the morning. And I have never been able to get that picture out of my head.

For when I eat spaghetti, I know the loggia lies freshly white-washed just outside the kitchen door. Whenever I eat in the more expensive Italian restaurants, everything looks so fake with all those Chianti bottles and plastic vines, in comparison to Enrico's chip shop. For all their pretensions, the exhorbitant trattorias don't feel like Italy, and Enrico's did.

I say it did, for it is all changed now. The last time I looked for the place I couldn't find it at first. Eventually, in place of the old marbled exterior, I found a modern Fish 'n' Chicken bar.

A sinking feeling grew in my stomach as I entered the Alcan doors. The place was retina-shattering bright. Working-class places usually are, as though the colour control knob has been turned up high. Everything was bright; the Formica, the glossy ceiling, the two young owners – and the fish frying machine. It sparkled at every point of its glass and steel frontage, at every lip of its Germanic, characterless, hulk. There was no vaguely Art-Deco opalescent glass with a square picture house clock set in it. And there was no picture of Naples Bay. A wave of despair swept over me. This was no triumphant ark, only a stainless steel coffin, with a darkness all around it, despite the glare.

The ark had gone, and so had Enrico and his stout little wife with the eyes like black coffee. They had gone back to Italy, to Naples, no doubt to sit in a quiet white-washed loggia high above the bay. God knows how often Enrico thought of that place as he looked at the picture and shifted the chips around. It must be difficult for him now, in a way, over in Italy, for he spent more than 30 years in a grey northern industrial city where it rained and grew dark as you came out of the pictures. And perhaps, you never know, he now sits out, in his place in the sun, and occasionally looks at a picture of a dark street somewhere in Glasgow with the street lights reflecting in the rain.

On the Wagon

YOUR MAN here is off the drink. It has been a changed Urban V all week. The eyes are, if not clear of a morning, at least visible. The rubicund complexion is fast disappearing. At this rate I shall start to look pale and interesting within the month, as pallid as Roderick Usher, and quite as sober. The slight rippling of fat around the collar shall diminish, and the waistline will be back to the 28 inches of my youth. I said waistline, lads. Why boast? In fact the only thing likely to increase is my bank balance. For a start, I shall no longer have to spend a fortune on Gold Spot. Quite the little boozer's pal, Gold Spot is.

For the benefit of those of you who are unacquainted with the above, it is the brand name of a well-known aerosol breath-freshener and is greatly employed by teachers, salesmen, chaps who 'meet the public', and senior civil servants who are unfortunate enough to advise teetotal senior ministers. Journalists never use such a thing. There is a reason for this. Only those who have not recently had drink taken can ever smell the breath of a toper. There is no such thing as an editor who has not recently had a drink taken.

Teetotallers are a dangerous lot though. I recollect a non-drinking headmaster who once had the misfortune to include me on his staff. He was convinced that I – along with half the staff – drank three bottles of meths every Friday lunchtime. This is because a teetotaller can smell even one wee half of beer from thirteen paces. The headie thought that the very breath of a breath on you signified alcoholism.

I thought I had him beat myself and dosed myself liberally with Gold Spot morning, noon – especially noon – and at four o'clock on the way out the school. I supplemented this with a steady diet of violet cachous. Unknown to myself the insane headmaster found the reek of peppermint and acacia emanating from my person so intense that for years he believed I had sunk to the gutter and was secretly consuming absinthe in my cupboard throughout the day. I could have got promotion if it hadn't been for a headie's ignorance in the matter of alcoholic effluvia. I coulda been a contender. Fate is like that though; he is a right bastard, and even worse than headmasters.

But now is different. I am off the sauce. The booze and me are finished for a while and John Barleycorn will just have to find another constant companion in the meantime. The liver is getting a rest and Morning is a changed woman altogether. (I always think of Morning as a young girl in a white dress with sunny eyes. Evening wears scarlet, and Night slips into a diamente bracelet and something more comfortable). Morning now sees me bright enough, and able to pass the notorious toothbrush test, which is to say that I can, with alacrity, brush the back molars without an involuntary – if that's the word – desire to throw up. It is surprising how rarely I cut myself shaving this weather. What is surprising really is how I cut myself shaving at all back in the old pre-sober days. I use an electric razor.

Giving up the bevvy is a sobering experience. Well of course it is. What I mean is that going off the drink is, so to speak, not all beer and skittles. For a start, it is extremely boring. It is only when you decide to forego even an infrequent small refreshment that you discover why teetotallers are the way they are. It is not for nothing that

Burns maintained that whisky and freedom gang thegither. Will Fyfe once put teetotallism splendidly. 'Ach!,' he said, 'when ye're teetotal ye've got a rotten feeling that everybody's your boss.'

Going on the wagon is fraught with frustrations. Where do you go to at nights? Aimless wanderings around streets or parks are bound to attract the attention of the police, especially if they have previously noted your continuous presence well after hours in half of Glasgow's boozers when they come in themselves 'just to check things out'. Do not give me drivel about jogging or bowls or joining bloody evening classes. And you know my views on telly-gawping. In truth, there is only one place you can relax when tense with sobriety: the pub.

It is then that you face the problem of what to replace the odd wee goldie with. You can try dreary concoctions with ginger beer and lemonade and lime cordial and after an hour of it you will soon realise why Colonel Gaddaffi and his pals are all mad dogs. They are positively inflamed, my dears, by Irn Bru and other such mineral waters. There is, I am sure you agree, nothing like a wee refreshment for putting things into proportion.

My solution is, I agree, hardly a solution at all. I simply wait until half past ten and upon that magic witching point I invite myself to a small libation. 'I don't mind if I do, Mr. McLean' I say to myself, and being a generous enough man and one always to stand his round I buy myself one back. Two drams a night can hardly be called bibacity. As in the case of the nailbiter who stops, the flood of unaccustomed virtue is a reward itself. And virtue will make a changed man out of anybody.

Friends of Mine

My Little Palace

IT WAS, understandably, a busy day in Heraghty's Bar – St Patrick's Day after all – and the chums were ready and waiting to see the Grand Slam game on my newly-acquired TV set, and it was me giving across the keys of my rather splendid flat to my brother Dick and me what was left to purchase the carryout. I reluctantly administered the keys.

'Don't' I said, 'make too much of a mess.' I slipped off to Oddbins and stuck I don't know how many cans of Pils into plastic bags and a few bottles of cheap red vino, and there was enough whisky in my house already to have done for a topping-out ceremony in the Gorbals circa the time that a miracle was going on and Sir Basil Spence was execrating the landscape for his knighthood and at the expense of Gorbalian commonsense. My chums went up to the magnificent apartment which I enjoy in the South Side of Glasgow. I invested in a bottle of Bushmills Malt.

I could tell the game was on, and that my pals were there, by the noise. A bit more too. Mrs Rowan next door alerted me. 'Jack,' she says, 'you should see the mess these boys have made. I telt them, but they just wouldn't wipe their feet.' I opened the door. Wipe their feet? By the look of the carpet they seemed capable of wiping almost any part of their anatomies, and especially on my carpet. They had obviously wiped themselves on the august rugs. I cracked up.

I made them go out to the hall and clear it up. I went into my living room, in which the television set was giving every Scottish rugby fan a heart attack. It was sod-all to my own cardiac situation. There were enough peanuts ground underfoot to have made up a shipment of peanut butter from a Jimmy Carter export company. Crisps were being trampled into my powder-blue flooring to the extent that, given another hour, it would have turned into a pitch that even a junior football team would have regarded less than playable. The chums were flicking ash off their King Edwards as if it was Friday night in the Cafe Royale in 1889 with Aleister Crowley at the head of the table, and kicking over tins of export beer. One chum – a noted Scottish psychiatrist, I might add – spat inexpertly into the fire. It was a gas fire too.

The blood quickened; the blood froze in fact. The scene before me was in keeping with the old days when I lived in squalor. Squalor it was too: I can yet remember wakening up of a morning and my bum sore because I had spent the night lying upon a saucepan of baked beans in my bed. The sudden realisation that I had not had beans for some days drew the fact that I had been cohabiting with an ageing pan of food for nights at a time. The discovery of a utensil with congealed fried eggs at the foot of the bed gathered an immediate conclusion that one had been drunk for days. Talking of days, changed it is this weather.

This weather I would sooner have Sir John Gielgud in my bed than a frying-pan. These days I have went over the top and am determined in my desire for a house which would do credit to the Duke and Duchess of Windsor in the Bois de Boulogne. Houseproud? If the toilet roll is put on the wrong way I am telephoning the council insisting on a visit from the Environmental Health. You should see me on the question of hygiene altogether. I couldn't give a blue fart about that ozone layer: I have been squirting the old fresh-air spray with sweet-pea scent round the ancestral home every three hours since I moved into my little palace.

Goddammit, I have practically turned into Syrie Maugham, let alone that old queen of a husband of hers, the dreadful Somerset, in my appalling demands on the homemaking sensibility. There are bon-bon dishes with delicately-hued sugared almonds in them. I make my cleaning lady polish the things with Pledge, for heaven's sake. I have stopped reading books because it buggers up the shelves and leaves an ugly space. The next thing is stopping wearing clothes as they have a shocking tendency to lie by themselves on the floor of a morning and upset my wakening aesthetic.

This is where Heraghty's Bar comes in, and not a moment too soon. I have got to the stage where my house is too beautiful for *me*, for Christ's sake, to visit, let alone a collection of hairy-arsed rugby fans, (including the psychiatrist). The proper place for such chaps, and maybe me myself, is a bar where they can do damage to somebody else's establishment. Even then, after the victory on Saturday, and the triumph of St Patrick's Day, and big Flockhart singing Rose of Tralee like a linty, even then, I made them use the ashtrays.

Friends Beside You

I AM a lucky fellow altogether: I have loads of chums and a zillion acquaintances, and I have used them dreadfully over the years. The weekly drivel you encounter each Friday is proof of that, for the pals are never off the column. The Von, Leo the Tim, Slick Nick, Big Cairnduff, Peetah, Jackie, Benny, Shug the Skirt, and many more; it is a lengthy cast list and I am not averse to jagging up my Friday movie with guest stars on the credits.

There are also those who have not made an appearance recently but who have regularly starred in the past. Frank McGuinness, the Man in Black, is less in evidence in public life these days, while Wee Tam, once a leading player, is now a respectable husband and father: not quite respectable enough to cease enacting the wondrously inebriated deeds which got him many a major role; respectable enough though to demand that his exploits go under a pseudonym in case his mother-in-law finds out.

Those who deplore my using of my very own pals are, I suspect, upset because they are too boring to merit a mensh, and they are wrong as well, because most people rather appreciate their names in the blatts, even in circumstances when they are shown as less than impressive. Anyway, if they are friends of mine they know well that I am a mendacious blabber-mouthed little shit in the first place, and just put up with it.

And a friend is somebody who, right on the bottom line, puts up with you and expects to have to. In a pal, you can have a right to expect loyalty to your faults, especially the ones which can't be ignored. A pal has his duty by you. Carrying ones pals home when they are slightly impaired by excessive refreshment is the least of it. The following, more dramatic, demands must equally be met: loyalty during impending police action due to the over cheerful behaviour of your comrades; the removal of said comrades' car keys when in such a condition; intervention should the possibility of fisticuffs be implicated even when the opposing protagonist is the size of Geoff Capes.

There are, however, certain situations in which chums can bloody well sink or swim. A slurred suggestion that you may wish to share a meal of ham and eggs made by the chum's spouse upon arrival by taxi at his establishment at one in the morning must be firmly rejected. Your pal can face his wife on his Jack Jones: you are sure to get nothing but trouble out of such an invitation. There are occasions when a buddy can just sway on his own two feet.

But then, such ephemera as wives, weans, any aspect of the extended family at all, have nothing whatsoever to do with classic male friendships. I have been best man, godfather, and pallbearer on behalf of chums, but that is only helping out the comrades responsibilities with a shoulder up and nothing more. Friendship is larger than that.

Emerson came out with something drippy about friendship. Said a pal was somebody you could be sincere with. Others will tell you that such a relationship as friendship requires respect for each other. Maybe both are true. I only know that in the twenty odd years that Von Flockhart and myself have been pals, for instance, we have scarcely uttered a civil word to each other. Overt approval of each other is regarded as anathema in male comradeship except in extremely maudlin circumstances, and each of my cronies tend to speak in tones of withering contempt for me and for each other, and we would not have it any other way.

But if I can admit to the possession of many amigos, and many a decent acquaintance, it was not always so. I suspect that is the reason why I collect pals the way some fellows do stamps. As a boy and youth I was without friends near enough. As a child I was smart-mouthed and precociously cynical, doubtless a defence mechanism for being so wee. There is nothing the adolescent boy prizes more than conformity, and I was distinctly lacking in that department though, God knows, I tried hard enough to be otherwise. It made misery in my heart which in turn caused me to be often wretched and silly and boastful which didn't help.

But, oddly enough, as I grew into man's estate I found that the very personality traits which had once kept me out of the gang were now rewarded with a wee invite to join up. The once-jejune misanthropy was now seen as glorious 'differenceness', the constant smart-mouthing viewed as patter. And, as I found my feet with friends I found that nobody else, even the guys whom I had admired for their ineffable ability to fit in, had never felt that they sort of belonged either. In short, as the lads got older they began to find the confidence to admit that they hadn't any, or anyway, not much.

Another paradox emerged. Many of those who once had seemed to fit so snugly and smugly no longer had a single chum left. Lots of them were the sort of chaps who stoutly maintained that their 'families came first'. You can see them yet, on their half-yearly soujourns down the pub looking vainly for friends they once had, flitting from boozer to boozer wondering where everybody has gone to. Such fellows console themselves with the notion of the bosom of their family. Just wait till the family grows up.

My Da, God rest him, stopped having pals after the War when he left the Army. I suppose in thirteen years as a squaddie pals had become a carousel in which people kept getting off without even a cheerio to leave behind them. I think myself he was the poorer for that. We kids were too, for your Dad's pals prepare you for your own.

But, prepared or not for pals, I have them now. The Von, Leo the Tim, Wee Tam, Big Cairnduff; stars all. And if the only movie you see them in is the one in the Friday column in this blatt, they are superstars in the big picture, the biggest one for me. And I intend to finish it off with the classic ending. When I ride off into eternity I want them riding beside me and into that last sunset.

Hotel Breakfasts

I WAS twenty-five when I first stayed in a hotel. And I stayed in it courtesy of the National Union of Students, for whom I was an Executive Member with, as my ex-NUS colleagues tartly recall, irresponsibility for everything. I remember though that I managed to persuade a young female student politician to come up to my room. Once there I thought hard. What does one do in a position like this *in a hotel*. I mean there must be something a little more plutocratic in hotels. So I picked up the 'phone and rang the desk. 'Night Clerk?' I asked, 'Send up a bottle of bourbon!' I pronounced the last as 'BURBAN'. I was entirely unprepared for the answer. 'F- off,' the night clerk said. I'll bet that never happened to Humphrey Bogart.

The idea of hotels really gets to me though. As a matter of fact I regularly take morning and afternoon coffee in

Glasgow's Central Hotel. Considering that you get three cups of coffee out of a pot for 50p, and you can sit in peace and quiet in old leather armchairs and sleep off the lunchtime booze, it is surely just ignorance that causes people to go to the bakery chains teashops. In earlier days when I first walked up the Central staircase I was filled with dread that they would know. 'They' were the snooty waiters who I thought would recognise real money when they saw it, and they would recognise me as bloody riff-raff the moment they clapped eyes on me, and have me ejected. Funny how you don't mind the bum's rush out of a scabby wee bar, but the thought of having your collar felt by a hotel flunkey makes the blood run cold.

Actually I got over that a long time ago, ever since I worked in hotels myself, not as a college job you understand, but as a fully paid-up flunkey, all white jacket, bow-tie, and posh accent upstairs, and bevy, oaths, and larceny downstairs. When I lived in London I used to regularly don the one suit I possessed and go and look at the Rich in the Hilton Hotel lounge bar. By then the feeling of dread had almost subsided. But if I had been Wee Tam, and I had experienced his sordid little saga, it would have taken somewhat longer for my embarrassment to fade away.

I wormed the story out of him not so long ago. It took a few small refreshments but eventually Tam confessed the lot. It is the kind of experience that you lock up inside yourself, to emerge occasionally late at night, and in your bed. I have got a few bad memories like it myself, including one which, until recently, I couldn't tell anybody, concerning an occasion when I read the wrong text out of the Bible at a Lifeboy concert, and realised to my horror that one of the words in the next sentence was going to be 'Shittite'. I have since woken up at four in the morning drenched in sweat, in a foetal position, my hands between my knees, moaning for

Our Lords Son, and seeing not only myself aged ten in a lifeboy jersey, but row upon row of parents in front of me and *that word* two lines down. But confession is, as they say, good for the soul, and Tam gave us the lot. It was curiously like a confession too, being held in the snug of Moore's Bar.

When Wee Tam was a lad of seventeen, (a rather improbable thought), he was apprenticed to a firm of insurance brokers. This was in the days when you could get a clerical job without having a PhD, and Tam was being groomed, at his tender age, for stardom. Accordingly, he was sent up to Aberdeen to learn the business. He travelled up from Glasgow with two elder colleagues, a man of about twenty-five, and an Area Manager in his early forties, and they all booked into the Station Hotel in Aberdeen. Not only was this the first time that Tam had been in a hotel, but it was the first time that he'd drunk a bottle of wine with his dinner, followed by brandy and liqueurs, and whisky in the hotel lounge. It was therefore a befuddled Tam who fell into his bed that night. It was a hot summer night, and Tam began to sweat horribly. He hauled off the quilt, then a blanket, then two more, and, to cut it short, Tam finally wrenched off his pyjamas, and lay there naked on top of an equally naked mattress.

Earlier in the day, Tam had ordered a cup of tea and a 'Glasgow Herald' (foolish boy!), for 7.30 the next morning. It was now 7.30 in the morning and Tam did not hear the chambermaid's knock on the door. It is a peculiarity of British hotels that the staff want you out of the room as quickly as possible, and indeed would greatly prefer you to give them a cheque and then spend the night somewhere else and not mess up the beds. Tam had ordered tea at 7.30, and by God he was going to be woken at 7.30. The chambermaid of course walked in on young Tam, who was stretched out on the bed, and being only seventeen was, shall we say, not only naked but er... rigid. Tam was rudely awoken out of his nightmares to find a worse one confronting him. 'Your tea and paper, Sir,' said the chambermaid, (an ageing lady by the way – none of your 'Men Only' fantasies here!), with all of the nonchalance of the hotel worker. Almost immediately realising his predicament Tam emitted a scream and, hurling the bedsheets about him like Ava Gardner in the movies, he promptly upset tea all over the bed. 'Dinnae worry Sir,' said the chambermaid patronisingly. 'Ye'd be surprised whit we see every day in hotels.' She mopped up the spilt tea with her towel. 'If ye were that warm, Sir, why did ye no open the windae?' she added. 'Why not indeed,' thought a pinker than usual Tam to himself. 'Ah widnae worry Sir,' reassured the chambermaid. 'Ye've no embarrassed ME!' And as she closed the door Tam could hear her peals of laughter ring down the corridor outside. Now if you add an early morning occurrence like that to a hangover you can understand that Wee Tam was not as perky as he might have been, as he hurried downstairs, already late for breakfast with his two superiors.

It was bright in the breakfast room, with the crisp white tablecloths glaring in the sunlight. Tam's bosses looked ruddy and fresh, in contrast to Tam's uneasy pallor. 'How do you feel this morning Tom?' asked one of them, to which Tam replied that he felt fine. The two were insufferable that morning, rubbing their hands together jocularly, slapping the palms, talking loudly, clanking teaspoons against a cup, which by the sound of it, Tam's ears may well have been the bell that deafened Quasimodo. The waitress appeared at the table and Tam was handed the menu. 'Remember,' said the manager cheerily, 'The Company is paying for this, Tom. Get a good breakfast inside you. Have the lot.'

Tam looked at the breakfast menu. He never had breakfast at all at home. And he had never seen such things for breakfast in his life. He had read P.G. Wodehouse though and he knew all about country house breakfasts – fried kidneys and bacon and kedgeree and all that. What the toffs had. 'I know you young chaps eat like horses,' the manager was saying, 'did myself at your age.' He was plumping his fat complacent hands together.

So Tam looked at the breakfast menu and ordered breakfast. It certainly seemed a lot but no doubt, he thought, the toffs always eat this way. He ordered fruit juice, and porridge with cream. There was a line under that and Tam went on to the next section, demanding kippers. He ordered bacon and eggs from the section below, and added scrambled eggs. He took toast and marmalade and a pot of tea, and finally asked for toasted bannocks. The two men looked at him strangely as they ordered their fruit juice and cornflakes.

By this time Tam was beginning to realise his error, but he couldn't admit it to his older colleagues, and in any case he couldn't possibly let them discover that he was suffering from a hangover as well. The waitress brought the porridge and the ordeal began. Tam managed to stagger down the lumpy gruel, and started on the kippers. Bone after bone came in every mouthful. It was like eating a box of dressmakers pins. Eventually he finshed and within seconds two thin rashers of pink bacon appeared on a plate, the grey fat quivering as he touched it with his fork. Two yellow egg yolks winked obscenely up at him. By now his colleagues were beginning to drum their fingers on the table. 'Tom, eh... we're running rather late you know.' By now too, the other customers were looking over at this amazing boy. Tom was oblivious to all in his agony.

The scrambled eggs came next, a pale yellow mound set in a little puddle of water like urine round a street lamp. Tam's arm ached with lifting the fork to his mouth. The breakfast room was totally silent, every eye in the place fixed on Tam. People were willing him to win, as they gazed open-mouthed in fascinated horror. The toast and marmalade was like a torture designed by Edgar Allan Poe. At each mouthful the pendulum swang closer till Tam could feel his flesh creep. Another mouthful. Tam couldn't tell if he'd swallowed it or not. He could imagine his entire intestinal tract, his throat, his gullet, his tonsils, packed with food. He began to envisage himself as an oddly shaped Michelin man crammed with cream buns and kippers and pale eggs. At last Tam finished, but the restaurant was still silent, the audience waiting for the final effort. A plate of bannocks, glistening with butter, floated onto the table-mat in front of him. Tam poured out another cup of tea. Just as he raised the tea-cup to his lips, out of the corner of his eye, Tam could see the little windows of the swing doors through which the waitresses came with the food. Both windows were filled with the amazed faces of the kitchen staff. Suddenly their expressions changed and their faces became suffused with laughter. Tam couldn't hear their mirth through the glass. But he could see in the centre of one of the windows, a finger pointing at him, a finger belonging to a figure obviously saying something to the other chefs and waitresses. With a chill going down his spine, Tam recognised the figure as his chambermaid of the naked encounter.

The next thing he remembers is that there was a sudden explosion as his superiors backed instantly out of their chairs. He remembers that he was standing up himself. A great jet of half-digested breakfast was thundering across the table. Tam was sick over the table, himself and over the Area Manager.

It was some years later that Tam ventured into hotels again. For one thing, he didn't have the money, what with being unemployed for so long. Nowadays of course Tam has learnt the trick of eating in restaurants and staying in hotels, or buying clothes in expensive shops. When he's sick at a restaurant now he calls the waiter over to clean up the mess. And if he meets a young chap he doesn't ply him with drink that the boy cannot cope with, and doesn't let him make a fool of himself. He shows the boy how to order a meal. He doesn't even wink at his friends behind the lad's back. I suspect it's more self-preservation than mere kindness. That way Tam doesn't end up being puked over.

As for the two insurance men, they somehow remind me of that word I was so scared to pronounce at a Lifeboy concert over twenty years ago. A right couple of shittites they were. Tam has got over his appalling experience in practical terms, and his recent confession has doubtless laid the ghost to rest at last. Mind you, even yet Tam rarely has breakfast, particularly in hotels. And come to think of it, what DOES bourbon taste like?

A Sporting Life

Do I Like Rugby?

I HAVE NEVER understood Rugby. I could understand the singing and dancing and bevvying which goes on in Edinburgh when there is a game on at Murrayfield but I could never understand Rugby as the reason for it. I mean, the game's so weird. The ball is a funny shape, and can't roll properly. You kick the ball *Over* the posts. The only way you can score with a kick is by sky-ing it, a practice regarded with derision in soccer. Then there are strange inexplicable scenes in which grown men – and I mean grown: these chaps are positive giants, my dears – stick their heads between two other grown mens arses and then push heavily against other fellows doing the same thing against them. Daftest of all is that you can't pitch the ball up the park and allow some Dennis Law-type poacher to grab a quick wee try. Rugby makes even less sense than other sports.

The first time I played it, and I can assure you I did not play it for long, I was a little lad. I was a small and thin little lad. I was the sort of small and thin little lad who would embarrass any parent. My mum was convinced that other parents were muttering things darkly like: 'They hardly feed that boy!' I was the sort of little lad who should not be playing Rugby at all. That's what the P.E. teachers thought too.

The first time I played Rugby I didn't understand the rules any more than I do now. A boy called Wilson Stoddart – or was it Stoddart Wilson? I forget which, anyway it was that sort of back-to-front name – punched me in the face when I tried to tackle him.

Recovering from the blow I smartly caught up with him and scudded him back. It took a bit of time for the Gym teacher to explain that young mister back-to-front name had delivered what was called a 'hand-off' and that it was quite legitimate. Whereas my unbridled retaliation wasn't.

I didn't want to play the bloody game anyway. In common with most of the Scottish working class, at least the central lowland proles, I thought Rugby was a game for fairies. Very rough fairies admittedly, but posh boys and the like. Snobs n' that. The game I wanted to play was that smooth, suave, sophisticated and silkiest of games, Association Football.

Play it I did too, and with a tanner ball I was, like most boys who were the littlest in the class, rather skillful and adept. Football is a game in which the wee ones could always beat the big boys. Up until a certain age that is. When I was fourteen and played my one – and only – trial I discovered the truth of it: I was simply no good at it and I never would be. All that teasing dribbling wizardry wasn't worth a damn when you started real football. For a start, the big boys never let you get the ball.

Strange things happen in life though. For all my contempt for Rugby lots of the chums played it, including my brother who was rather ludicrously known in Rugby circles as 'Dancing Dick', and the Von who was a forward and whose only dancing was committed on the faces of his adversaries. My psychiatrist is also a rugger-bugger as well as an Italian. Actually he is not really my psychiatrist but he wants to be so that he can screw money out of me. If I ever think of going to a rugby-playing Italian psychiatrist who comes from Kirkcaldy then I will definitely need my head examined.

Other chums who play that ruffians game for gentlemen, as it is oft described, include Big Ches who I am told plays with his head – he nuts his opponents – and Big McCallum who doesn't have a head anyway as it is just another shoulder. They are a motley crew. But what I am trying to tell you is that I have been watching the Rugby on the box with several of the chums for over a decade now and have never understood it, try as I might. Until, that is, last Saturday. Last Saturday was the breakthrough.

Because last Saturday as I watched the glorious Scotland versus those Welsh blokes, I recognised a rule, well an infringement of one. Before Dancing Dick, before the Von, or the Italian psychiatrist, or anybody else, before in fact Bill McLaren himself, I spotted that a Welsh player had played the ball when on the ground when he should have released it. I casually pointed this offence out to the chaps which is to say that I screamed at the top of my voice that the asterisking Welsh asterisk had committed an offence of considerable asterisking dimensions. As I basked in my glory at this feat and bathed in the pals astonishment another little notion suddenly dawned upon me. That I liked Rugby.

As a former football fanatic who took in a game every Saturday in life but stopped going several years ago it is possibly understandable to other people. It is a revelation to me. I feel as though the scales have been dropped from my eyes. What could ever be more exciting than the ball passing down the line of backs leaving the wing to go hell for leather and fly – literally – across the line? What can be as satisfying a sporting sight as the loops and dazing patterns made by Scotland's current stalwarts? As thrilling as wee Laidlaw propelling his body and the ball out of the scrum? The list is endless.

Wait till we play those English chaps next week. There will be the pals, including the mad Italian psychiatrist, and me waiting for the half-time pies warming in the oven, beer cans proliferating and all of us raving in front of the TV set as Scotland prove their ineffable superiority. And after next week there is the World Cup when we will be doing the business to everybody, including this time, the Frogs. I may not even yet understand many of the rules. But I now understand the passion and go along with that.

The Old Firm

THERE HAD BEEN an atmosphere of impending violence all day. The town centre of Culture City had been thronged with mobs of youths chanting obscenities, pushing shoppers out of their path, occasionally encountering rival groups at which both sides indulged in taunts designed to lead to open fighting. Youths – and grown men too – had came from all over Scotland for this occasion. They had come from Aberdeen and Brechin and Edinburgh, and specially from the sectarian strongholds, the small tight towns of Lanarkshire and Ayrshire where the white trash live out their banal lives with an equal level of Buckfast and bigotry. This is the big one; the big day.

They had chanted vilely on buses and stoned the odd window, invaded the boozers that would let them in and weren't shut for the day. Now it is five o'clock and I am standing talking to the proprietor of one of Glasgow's smartest wine bars. We are hardly having a quiet chat over the bar. We are standing at the door of his shop where he is staying to keep out the savages who are now already fighting in the streets. His wife is inside, white and anxious, wondering when the bottles come through the tall bright windows of the cafe, advising customers not to go just yet, wait a bit until the mobs have passed through the city centre or are getting violently drunk in the pubs. A party of Australians had seen some of the rioting and now sat round a table, visibly shaken. Said football manager Billy McNeil in the pre-match programme: 'I have yet to see anything that remotely approaches the match for atmosphere and grandeur.' The match is probably the most famous club game in the world. Rangers and Celtic: the Old Firm.

What the Rangers-Celtic clashes are famous for is not the football, which is generally of a low standard, because the tensions of the occasion usually preclude good football. What they are famous for is the climate of sectarian and atavistic hatred, and for the ensuing violence. Few decent people now go to these matches, at least not without considerable apprehension. Were they to attend such games they will see gangs of thirty and more strong, battling with each other. Weapons are even used, broken bottles even more so. Buses which pass by are stoned. The police seem powerless in the face of it all. A little way along from the smart wine bar a bottle had been thrown from a bus, hitting a passing boy of twelve who was taken to hospital. There was a young boy in the cafe who asked if he could hide. This is the atmosphere and grandeur.

There was more of the same atmosphere and grandeur during the actual game, in the stadium. The fans are fenced in of course and the police now look only on the crowd. The days of a handful of big highland polis watching the match themselves and chatting with the supporters have gone long ago. Let us take a little look at the grandeur on the field of play. Let us look at Mr. Graeme Souness.

Mr. Souness has been player/manager of the Rangers club for just over a year, during which time he has undeniably brought success to the club. He has also been sent off three times over that year, and the last occasion was last Saturday.

Mr. Souness is a grown-up man of thirty-three. He was booked early on for dissent against the referee. At thirty-three even Mr. Souness should have grasped that the referee is in charge and that there is no game at all without the rules. The ageing football star then embarked on a dangerous foul which would have earned a sending-off even if he had not been booked first. Later, it is alleged, he swore horribly to the (unpaid) referee, and then repeated his foul language in front of another official. Mr. Souness is thirty-three.

Other players were guilty of acts of provocation, players from both sides. A Rangers player – clearly aged eight –

refused to shake hands with a Celtic player. So much for sport. But Souness is the team captain, and the manager, and responsible for the behaviour of his team. There is no excuse for his conduct on Saturday considering the nature of this particular match. It undoubtedly helped to create much of the ensuing violence, and I lay the blame for many of the injuries suffered by even innocent victims at the Rangers manager's door. In short I believe that Souness should be suspended from playing football for life. The only player to have been suspended sine die – Willie Woodburn – seems to have committed less of an offence.

But then I would suspend the match itself – sine die. Or at the very least, if it MUST be played, it should be behind locked gates without a thug, except of course for some of the players, in sight. I am all for civil liberties but there are several activities – and I name the Orange parades as one of them, (please note: I am not a Roman Catholic), – which limit the liberties for the majority of us. I don't know what to do about the creatures who disrupt our lives at such times, anymore than you do. But I do not believe that the opportunities for their vile behaviour should be permitted in the first place.

The Camanachd Cup

I AM DEFINITELY your man for the scenery. A good dod of scenery and a few wee halfs to go with it and what more could an aesthete like myself want? Thus it was that when the Camanachd Cup boys suggested I may wish to have a squint at the shinty cup final in Fort William, I jumped at the chance. In the case of shinty cup finals scenery, like freedom, and whisky gang thegither. The only sensible way to witness scenery however is through glass, either through a car window or a hotel one. Highland scenery might look breathtaking but it can be injurious to health. If the fresh air doesn't get you, the midges will. The midges of Fort

William are said to come armed with claymores, and other blood-curdling war cries.

The car window was easy enough and was supplied by Mr. Archie Hind which is to say that the distinguished novelist agreed the night before, doubtless while in drink, to come along for the trip and drive us both up to the Highlands. We pledged to start at eight the Saturday morning. This was a wise move. You must allow yourselves an hour and a half extra on a Saturday morning. If Archie and myself had suggested a reasonable hour the only shinty we'd have seen would be in Heraghty's Bar.

It was a cold dreich morning but that didn't matter as we swept along the winding road which hugs Loch Lomond. I nearly forgot my hangover as I uttered little shrieks, my dears, of delight at the bluebell-infested forests we were going through. (On this last observation, it has always seemed to me that the bluebell should be Scotland's national emblem rather than the grisly thistle). By the time we got to the end of the loch I was practically greeting with the beauty, (and the hangover), and felt a little like a Caledonian Godfrey Winn.

A shinty match would not be the place for such bluebells as the late Mr. Winn. Let me paint the picture clearly for you. Shinty is played in a big sodden field and the piercing wind comes hurling itself down from the snowy heights of Ben Nevis and the driving rain sears the face and the midges can still get at you and in the meantime a collection of big meaty tcheuchters hit you with sticks. There is a ball about somewhere for some of the time. Watching shinty is not much less arduous than playing it. I was wearing a smart blazer, white ducks, and a coupon blue with the cold. There was nothing for it but the charms of the beer-tent.

Some beer tents are dreadfully suave affairs. The Highlanders don't go in much for suaveness: it is the alcohol which attracts. The beer tent at Fort William was of a size just big enough to house Colonel Ghaddaffi and maybe one of his wives, but no bigger. It was surprising, in the end alarming, to discover how many thirsty highlandmen could cram themselves in. It was the Tardis with drink.

Suitably fortified with some of the amber fluid I went out to watch the match. It was half time and the Lochaber Junior Pipe Band were out in force and very good they were too, led as they were by Pipe Major Moira Morrison. You don't expect girls to play the pipes, but they did and very good they were too. Doubtless they will be playing shinty next. A charming small girl named Morna said I was to mention the drummers as well, oh, and also herself. Well I have.

Intending to move back to the hotel to get a warm to myself I chanced upon the Glenmorangie chaps who were sponsoring the match. A small select group of newshounds were around talking in a desultory way to Sir Russell Johnstone and clearly hoping for a wee half to be slapped into their mitts. I got one myself but it was all with a certain reluctance I thought. There was a faint note of 'You'll have had your tea?' about the hospitality. The newshounds were complaining bitterly under their breath about the whisky company's parsimony, which I may say is unusual at these affairs.

In some previous years the cup final has been held in Glasgow and the teams and their supporters stay up till dawn. This year they went home early to carouse in their native heath, which was a pity because the apres-shinty is three-quarters of the fun. This did not stop a bit of carousing ourselves with a bunch of boys from the Glasgow University Shinty Club, one of whose number was a big lad called Alan who came from Easterhouse. As far as I could see Alan and his mates were spending their grants in one night. I don't know about them but the next morning myself and Archie felt as though we had been beaten with camans by a team of Highland polis. Later in the day we stopped at the wonderful Kilmartin Hotel where we were entertained by the troops. This time the camans were electrified. A weekend of scenery and the drink it was. I am still recovering from the both.

The Blame of Those ye Better

AS IN ALL tragedies the one at the Hillsborough Ground was scarcely reported to the nation but blame was being readily apportioned. It is a natural desire on the part of human beings to bring blame into it: a means perhaps by which disaster can be comprehended. Thus it is that after every railway accident the authorities are accused of niggardliness in the safety procedures and the authorities respond by hinting that the driver or the guard or the signalman may have been at fault. Just as long as somebody is seen to be found guilty. At Hillsborough we have seen a flurry of blame; the police for not controlling the crowds; the football authorities for their allocation of tickets; even the ground itself for being too small. It is misplaced blame if you ask me.

One of the problems about this latest football catastrophe is that the public mind is more than a touch ignorant of the factors involved. The majority of the populace never, or almost never, go to a football match. The overwhelming majority of women for instance have seen no more than a couple of matches in their lives. It is hard for them to contemplate the circumstances which pertain at a game. It is hard for non-initiates into this mystery to grasp what a football crowd is like.

But ask any regular football devotee what it is like trying to get out of a ground at the end of a game and he will tell you. If he is a sensible man he will tell you that he waits for about quarter of an hour before he takes his leave. Because when you are coming down those steep staircases two minutes after the final whistle you are almost always in a position of risk. The momentum of the hordes will carry you along, your feet hardly touching the ground at all. Big grown-up men can find themselves off the ground entirely, their mass floating with the crowd. Cries of 'Watch the weans' or 'Mind the wife' are all about you. Older fans totter unsteadily as the fans push behind. The amazing thing is that so few disasters actually occur.

This is of course what happens at football matches. It never happens at cricket matches. Or at Rugby or Hockey or race meetings. Anybody who has ever gone to Murrayfield will know that the ground is dreadfully unsafe. The reason why such horrors as Ibrox or Heysel and now Hillsborough don't happen at Murrayfield is simple and everybody knows it. The reason why you can pack the place with over-excited screaming schoolgirls for a Hockey international and emerge without incident is simple too. It is that the fans and supporters know bloody well how to behave themselves. I have been to Murrayfield for an international with half the fans howling with alcohol and I have never seen an angry word between supporters, never seen a bottle fly, never seen a crush. I have seen schoolgirls near delirious with excitement at a hockey game and never witnessed a sign of crowd unrest. It is different with football.

For the plain and simple fact about the blame for this latest tragedy is that it is the fans who must shoulder it. It is the football fans themselves. And every regular football-goer knows it too. It was not the Football Association who turned up in their droves without tickets. It wasn't them who got out of control outside the ground. It wasn't the police who pushed and shoved at the back and didn't care about anybody else. No policeman shouted and bayed and pushed and shoved. The crowd outside would not be capable of policing. If you have ever been to a Rangers and Celtic game you will know what I mean when I say that it can be utterly impossible to control a crowd unless you have got one police constable to every three fans.

Sure, it isn't every fan that behaves badly. But it is a hell of a lot of fans who do all the same. Even now, despite the ban on alcohol in Scottish grounds you will find the same mindless savagery which characterises much of the younger support; you will find the same paean of hatred directed towards opposing fans at almost every football match, no matter how humble. For the fans caused Hillsborough as they cause headaches for everybody outside of their own cult. To blame the police reminds me more than a little of the blame directed towards a schoolteacher when a class gets out of hand. The children aren't to be faulted for running amok, for telling the teacher to fuck off. The teacher is the guilty party. It is always the teacher, or the police or the authorities or the ones up there. It is never the miscreant himself.

Over the last thirty years we have seen the lessening of authority in the home, at school, and in the public domain. Much of this was surely right. Some of it wasn't. While most football fans remain decent and polite a large minority are selfish to a degree unacceptable to the population as a whole. Me. Just me. Nobody else. I have to get in. Sod you. The kind of thick and self-centred hooligans that I once tried to teach: dear God I could see them at Hillsborough all right, pushing just to be there first. But that is one half of what happened in Sheffield last Saturday.

The other half is that these people with their impoverished lives have made a fetish of football. A game, essentially for boys has become a totem for the dispossessed. That is why Rugby games or schoolgirl hockey matches or race meetings do not excite such incidents as occur at football matches. The fans in these other games know they are games. They are not really that important. Neither, as Hillsborough teaches us once again, is football.

The Boat Race

I SAY OLD MAN, I mean, what? One knows the jolly old
Empire wasn't what it was: these Government chappies
have seen to that what with some ageing club waitress
running the show and a host of chaps who remind one of
those coves you see parading about the lower class of
drapers being Cabinet wallahs but I say it's a bit much.
There was your Urban Voltaire set for fun and a weekend of
vigour and what not at the jolly old Boat Race and a chance
to sport the old silver and black neckwear of one's alma
mater and looking forward to it too. I gave my man express
instructions to lay out the beige suitings and the silver grey
for the journey and negotiated with the bank for a sum
sufficient to keep your correspondent in the manner to
which he intended to be much accustomed over the
weekend. It was a svelte – I think that's the word – Urban
V who stepped lightly onto the Flying Scot at the station of
a Friday morning. A dashed fine morning it was too. Sun
was up and the sky was as blue as a film star's eyes.

I had rather looked forward to a spot of the old e. and b.
as a breakfast treat. The railroad used to do an especially
good breakfast. I spied the collation they were purveying – a
ghastly affair with those foreign roll things – and an
omelette and fried potatoes. For breakfast for heaven's sake.
A stern whisky and soda seems to be the only alternative. I
do not mind admitting it. There are occasions when the
inner self yearns. It is, after all, five hours to London from
our little part of North Britain. I spent a good two hours
imagining the snowy napery and gleaming cutlery, not to
mention the spot of turbot meuniere with a glass of the best
fizzy to wash it down. A gooseberry tart with cream and a
decent Stilton should, I thought, complete the thing. Sadly
it was not to be. A surly steward with a Mancunian accent
informed me that lunch was off. Said it was the holidays.
Even suggested a beefburger. With, he said, relish. I could

see the relish in him. Chap probably dreams of the sheer delight in disappointing those of the elite such as myself. Also, the train was late.

Well, I mean to say, a chap braves the Easter weekend travel and finds himself without brekkers AND lunch. Can't grasp, myself, why public holidays require one to starve. Doesn't seem to make much sense somehow. But there you are. The English like to celebrate by closing everything down. They are most determined in this respect and especially at Easter. Very religious the English are. Renowned for it in fact. So there we are; no jolly old lunch and a small whisky costing a fortune. Not to worry, I thought, the Metrop beckons. There will be muffins still for tea and a good beefsteak and a drop of the old amber fluid in the Garrick. I sat back, lunchless, and gazed at the dispiriting views of Preston factories and the like.

It was a glorious afternoon in London and after a wash and brush up in my club I repaired to the bar for a quick one. You have guessed it: it was closed. 'It is the holidays' snorted the club steward who then explained in that patient way one's old schoolmasters adopted when talking to imbecilic youths. 'Right Ho.' I said and legged it for a couple of clubs where I could look forward to the whisky and soda and a few words with old cronies about the impending Boat Race. Well, I mean to say, your Urban V here is not entirely up in this English ritual and a few chaps from the respective academies in question should surely sort of, well, build up the atmosphere, if you know what I mean. Give one a taste for it. I found to my consternation that both the Savile and the Garrick were closed. The night before the big race too. Bit of a swizz all round, I thought it.

But not nearly as much of a swizz as the fact that the pubs weren't open till seven that night and – I reeled as I heard the news – closed at ten. I felt a little like the chap we were celebrating at Easter; a bit deserted in fact. This was not helped by what seemed like an hour waiting for a chum outside of the old Museum Tavern. It's right across from the British Museum. It too was closed. The holidays I expect. Well, what with one thing or another the jolly old ambience of pre Boat Race seemed sadly lacking. It was also a Friday night of sobriety I have not indulged in for twenty years.

But nothing dims the voltairean spirit. Morning saw me, if not bright eyed at least merely pinkish around the beadies. A tinkering with the kedgeree not to mention a kipper or two and a goodly dose of the Darjeeling saw me to rights and by that time the photog chappie had been announced into the presence I was feeling utterly tickety-boo, raring to go, have at them and that sort of rot. I don't know if you have ever encountered an expatriate Glaswegian press snap-taker – and one who has foresworn strong liquor to boot – before, but it is certainly an experience. Arthur was of a mind to enjoy alcohol by proxy, and, allied to the natural insanity of photogs anyway – there is a saying that goalkeepers are daft, there is even one that states that band drummers are certifiable: I can assure you that a press photog is a master in the field of lunacy. All I can tell you is that by the time I hit the august Winchester House Club where the press conference concerning this – and I was by now well aware of it – quite pointless exercise in British tradition, I was by no means requiring the glass that cheers. Arthur it has to be said, was urging me on in my efforts. I have seen the results. It is the first time in my experience that a press camera was focussing better than it's subject.

But here I was in the Winchester Club and here were all sorts of coves clad in blazers and the grey flannel. Beefeater Gin sponsor this race these days and they stinted the G & T not a whit, not to mention the Bucks Fizz. I am not sure I should be saying this but it appeared to me that our Rowing Correspondent was a touch eager in the matter of his encounter with the Champers. Our Rowing Correspondent I had imagined as a rum sort of cove, you know, six feet-eight with pectorals like buttocks on him and clad in a striped blazer. Our Rowing Correspondent turned out to be a chap my size in an M & S sweater who hadn't seen a razor for twenty-four hours or more and who speaks in the sort of tones one associates with a St. Aloysius old boy down on his luck. Our Rowing Correspondent seemed to know every other Rowing Correspondent and a frightful looking crew they appeared to be. Distinctly shady I should say.

But at least the chappies in charge of the Race were our sort – I beg your pardon – my sort. The fellow who welcomed the gentlemen of the Press didn't have mere marbles in his eppiglottis: Lord Elgin had brought them back from Athens by the sound of it, and he had a blazer with buttons like medals on it. The umpire was called Sweeney and spoke in a Birmingham dialect. It's always the same: the chap who knows most about sport comes from the less salburious areas of our land. I don't know why.

This is not entirely true. I had words with none other than the most famous figure of recent years in this rowing business, Dan Topolski. It was he who figured in the wonderful scandals of last year. A very pleasant chap too and what is more seemed genuinely interested in the sport. I will tell you this, and I found it amazing. It appears that these rowing blokes don't actually think much of the Oxbridge encounter. Seems that the Boat Race is more a jamboree for the Hooray Henries than it is a rowing contest. A bit of a spot of British liturgy rather than real sport at all. Well, I suppose the same could be said, sort of, about a Rangers-Celtic game.

I will say this for the Winchester House Club; it is a decent old establishment. Wood-panelling and that. Chap told me that it had been Cromwell's old HQ during that bit of bother the Anglo Saxons had back there. Lots of tradition and all that. In fact, I spied a couple of Beefeaters wandering about. They looked about twenty and deliciously lissome with long blonde hair. Girls as well which was a bonus. I supposed them to be representatives of the purveyors of Mother's Ruin. Everybody knew each other and all the old boys were having a spiffing time. They were all called 'Tom' or 'George' and wore ostentatious sweaters with stripes around the yoke. Over the smoked salmon and the fizz they were saying, uttering things like: 'I say, old boy, is the umpah actually heah.' Outside, the police brass band was giving us 'Land of Hope and Glory'. I spied an elderly naval gentleman standing downstairs discussing the finer points of sculling no doubt, with a London skinhead. Not for the first time did I wonder what kind of race the English are.

With the impending excitement and so forth I thought it about time to meet the lieges in the street. One of the lieges thus encountered was none other than the most famous henpecked hubby in Britain, Denis, he of 10 Downing Street.

I had encountered him before at the club and had been warned off actual speech with him by a senior exec. of the Beefwitted Company on the basis that the gentlemen of the press were too vulgar and would probably start asking questions about the colour of his wife's knickers.

Denis seemed to possess no objection whatsoever concerning the notion of Gin and Tonic and to the distress of the Home Office wallahs expressed the view that Oxford were his chosen champions. He also said that Glasgow was a dashed fine place. I have set aside a bottle of the white spirit in Heraghty's little club for his next visit.

You will know by now that the Boat Race is mainly to do with – whatever the young poseurs of London's stock market, who were much represented, think – the promotion of Beefeater Gin.

To this end two young ladies dressed in Beefeater uniforms with the most *exiguous* skirts agreed to take my arm as I assisted them to the boats. I have seen the photographs. I look like a doddering ancient being put to bed by showgirls.

It was then that the Blues, both Dark and Light, came out. They were all eight-foot-six with pectorals like armchairs and chattered freely with the press. This, I thought, was surprising. Just try talking to the players in, say, an Alloa-Brechin match. You will have words no doubt but will hardly be able to repeat them in print.

I was inexorably drawn to consider the original chaps who had started the entire affair back in 1829. What splendid surnames they had enjoyed. Oxford had Toogood, which was too good to be true, and Carter, Arbuthnot, Bates, and Staniforth, while good old Granta had Merrivale, Selwyn, Warren, Heath and Entwhistle.

The last few years has seen oarsmen with the most unlikely titles, most of them American sounding. Well, the lads went to it with a will, I must say, and so did we in the splendid confines of the Thames Rowing Club.

Everybody watched the race on the television save a large and corpulent gentleman in a pink and lavender striped blazer who had over-lunched and had fallen asleep with his head in a plate of salmon mayonnaise. 'Does it every year,' said a local. 'Last year it was cold curry,' he said.

The race seemed to be over dreadfully quick. I mean to say, these chaps have been training for yonks and there is practically a squillion quid spent on the jamboree by TV companies and it lasts about 20 minutes and anyway Oxford always win. Of course what we are all hoping for is some marvellous drama in which both teams sink and the coxes do the decent thing and shoot themselves with revolvers in the Ibis Boat Club.

This year only two dramatic instances seemed to occur. One was when one of the large oarsmen in the Cambridge boat broke it by being too big for it, and the other was when another Cambridge fellow caught a crab. I have known a few spirited young students in my days to catch crabs but not when rowing. It was *most* bemusing.

But Boat Race Night is even more legendary than the race itself. It is when mass battles centre on Piccadilly and the Vine Street police go into action. It was when that old rip, Harold MacMillan no less, demanded that the chaps 'go out and generally break up the town'. He had more to ask. 'If Piccadilly Circus stands tomorrow,' he said, 'I shall be disappointed. If Eros has not been moved or draped with suitable decorations, it will not have been a good night.'

I may say that the young Englishmen of today have overdone the spirit of irresponsibility. What I saw following the race wasn't a kick off from what the young blades get up to in Marbella of a summer's eve. Had it been dear old Glasgow and youths of proletarian history we would have called it hooliganism.

And, mind you, the pubs were shut. It was, after all, the holidays. Never mind the pubs shutting. Chaps like your Urban V are nonplussed by such disasters. We found a splendid little sculling club before the Dove opened its doors. At last we found sanity in this little hostelry, once the haunt of Dickens and Thackeray. It was packed full of Scots and Irish, none of whom knew the result of the race and who cared but little.

It was late when I toddled off back to my club. En route I had been ripped off in a taxi, been overcharged in a Chelsea restaurant, and accosted by a raging, and presumably blind, old queen. In the club an inebriated old chap touched me for two quid. I shook off the gloom and ordered another small libation. The bar, the steward told me, was closed. It is the holidays, he said.

The Establishment

The Man Who Should be King

SIR JACK McLEAN hardly suits, I think. Diminutives rarely do when it comes to a knighthood. Being an actual Lord is okay; Lord George Brown sounded tickety-boo, like Lord George Hell out of Oscar Wilde. Sir Oscar would have been all right too, if he hadn't blotted his shirt tail. Sir Jack is just daft. Lord McLean would have done if it wasn't that there are so many of them, ranging from near-century-old divines to a fair old swatch of aged war heroes who have been educated at Marlborough and the like. Myself, I have occasionally thought of buying an allotment on the isle of Muck so that I could get called the Lord of it. I suppose I will just have to be a knight all the same: contributions to public life, literature, education, or the distilling industry.

As it happens there are few and far between who get any kind of mensh in the Honours List at all for their contributions to anything other than that to the coffers of the companies which support the Conservative Party and All It Stands For. The above statement is probably close to a libel and our lawyers will want to take it out except that I am going to write the following paragraphs in such a way that it will not be possible to adopt such a course without making greater nonsense of the column than is usually permitted. Here is a worse calumny: nobody gets knighted unless they have done something which some of the people think grand and some of the others think despicable. Such was the case with the Bold Baron of Fordell, Mr. – now Sir – Nicholas Fairbairn.

I am indebted to the correspondent who suggested that Sir Nick was no more due a knighthood than your Urban V here was and I shall be looking for the old sword across the shooder in the next year or so. Said our correspondent: ' if being an aged, reactionary old dandy with a taste for drink' got Baron Fordell a dubbing then, argued this sensible chap, none other than myself should equally be the recipient of such an honour. But, as I say, Sir Jack had not got quite the right ring. It is too proletarian by half.

Sir John sounds the part, as I swan into the best hotel in Karlsbad, but as it happens my real name isn't John at all and it would sound foolish to my ears and I am damned if I am going to use my baptismal name just for a knighthood as I haven't been able to answer to it in my life. I know Sir Alf Ramsay had no bother responding to being Sir Alf but if you were called something as lumpen as Alf you would let yourself be known as anything at all. I am not going to be Sir Jack: I am holding out for a peerage. One of those hereditary ones at that.

I have never quite understood why anybody allows one of the wee daft honours to be attatched to themselves. I mean a CBE or an MBE or a Companion of Honour or all of that rubbish. Simple postmasters or mistresses get given that for rattling out postage stamps for eight decades, or the sort of Local Government servant who allows himself to spend forty years in the Sewage Department counting the flow of Regional turds and being what we call a public servant when what we mean is a drudge paid sod all but respected for not complaining about it. Sometimes we give honours to crippled folk because their legs don't work but they complain even less than the officials in the Sewage Works...

But there are other occasions when we get it right and award, at the end of the day, honour where honour is due. All these marvellous captains of industry who Provide Work For the People of This Country. And a few quid for themselves. I suspect there is cynicism at work here but I will try to keep a straight face. I am talking of the numerous honours which have gone out to the collection of spivs over the years and who have frequently ended up in the dock or anyway in the bankruptcy court. It is at such a time that one has a certain sympathy for the Queen, God Bless Her. If it was up to Her I suspect a cudgel across the shoulder blades would be more like it.

Far be it from me to comment upon the appropriateness of national honours but it does seem to most of the denizens of this land that there are not a few nonentities, as well as scoundrels, who are marked out in this manner. Not a few sycophantic academics come in for distinction where none exists within their own field. In academic life an honour is tantamount to being known as a bloody mountebank and those with a decency to them reject it.

Apart from Sir Nicholas Fairbairn the other Scottish-based worthy to arouse comment in his knighthood must be Sir Reo Stakis... doubtless for his contributions to cuisine. Thatcher government saw fit to advise Her Majesty that a knighthood was in order. This, in my view, gives rise to an entirely new philosophic, not to mention epicurean, movement: Sirreoalism. To award, the man who in my view has been the greatest force for the sort of fast food boil in the bag rubbish which now characterises Scottish restaurants, with a bloody knighthood rather than a brickbat is the height of Sirreoalism and I don't care if he came across here with only enough lace to fit round one leg of Mrs. Thatcher's knickers and dragged himself up by her suspenders either. Our correspondent was scathing about Nicholas Fairbairn – who as it happens was possibly the greatest Scottish QC in the post-war years – and about myself and I am doubtless due his scorn. In comparison to most of the others on this list of yearly shame I am practically the Man Who Should Be King.

By-Election Fever
WHAT A SPLENDID jamboree lies before us; especially before the hack of the species. The London scribes will be up in their droves infesting the vestibules of The Holiday, The

Hospitality, and The Albany. I hope Ken McCulloch can keep them Out of Devonshire Gardens. That is not all. There will be enough camera teams about George Square and the Merchant City to film GONE WITH THE WIND. Twice.

And if you think the above will be crowded, I tell you this: if you live in Govan you would be well-advised to get your messages in now because you will not be getting into the shops for tripping over cables and being interviewed by Malcolm Wilson. It'll be Lights, Camera, Action, for a month at least. If you are a wee woman in a shabby coat who eternally carries a net bag you would do better to move in with a pal on the other side of the city because the TV wallahs will have you interviewed to a frazzle. If you are a rough looking cove with scars on your coupon and faintly resemble Johnnie Stark out of NO MEAN CITY you should emigrate. The London boys will have your liver dancing with all the free booze they will be jagging down your throat while they film typical Govanites in typical Govan bars. It will not be all that easy these days to find an air raid shelter but if there is one left in Govan the telly chaps will gather every jakie they can find in the city and film them swigging bottles of cheap red biddy. Great ones for finding a bit of local colour the telly boys are.

The posh Sunday blatts will be enjoying a positive revelry of Govan analysis in which they will get everything subtly wrong. (Sweet Heaven, I could write one just now myself.) Govan will be a depressed part of the city in which the 'Miles Better' campaign has never set foot. There will be deserted shipyards with a lone, black crane as testimony to the decaying industrial landscape. (At this point Jimmy Reid will be exerting his swarthy bulk in front of a camera crew and talking great gobs of tendentious sentiment about being a Clyde-built man – 'This is where they made men...' he will be repeating, over and over again. I will bet there will be lots of lovely, revealing stuff about The Rangers, the Orange Lodge, and the Proddy bigotry. I will guarantee that they film outside two schools – one Catholic and one non-denominational where they will film some Asian children. 'Yet, for Govan, there are sweeping changes...' There will be shots of ageing yuppies throwing roast pheasants down them in the North Rotunda as the bleak wastes of the once-active shipyards make up the background. It'll be hard to do because the view from the Rotunda is rather splendid but, trust me chaps, they will find a way. The worst bits, though, will be the interminable recollections by boring old jossers about when Govan was practically a country in its own right. (Govanites go on about their area worse than Andy Cameron does about Rutherglen.)

Did I say that would be the worst? Never fear. The very nadir will be the frequent appearances of the candidates themselves. I have a feeling that it is probably just as well that Bob Gillespie was chosen for Labour on Wednesday back there because at least one of the Labour short leet made Johnnie Stark of NO MEAN CITY look cultured, and another talks smarter than Bernard Levin. Mr Gillespie is standard trade union issue and won't upset you too much on the box, as long as he keeps the, surely embarrassing, tattoos on his fingers out of camera range.

The Tory boy was recently described as a local lad which is surprising because he hails from Burnside which is about as local to Govan as Brechin would be, but in any case young Mr. Hamilton has as much chance of being elected as a spoilt paper. Yet another young chap commends himself to me. I would be sorely tempted to vote for a chap called Ponsonby at any election. The self-styled Democrats would do well to advise young Bernard to change his name. A Ponsonby for Govan simply will not do. I doubt if a Ponsonby has passed through Govan in fifty years.

But the media will not be bothering all that much with any of the above. The media are going to live in Jim Sillars pockets. Short of seeing Jim going to the lavvy, I think you can expect our hero to get more press coverage than the Pope gets on Good Friday. If I am not mistaken, Mr. Sillars will rise to the task. Notwithstanding the misgivings about his political judgement since he founded the ill-fated S.L.P., there is no denying that Jim could talk the hind legs off Red Rum and persuade you to spend a cold winter's night throwing snowballs at the moon. If Margot starts in on the act you might as well switch off the telly: they will be on more often than Wogan, and it'll be igloos you are tossing at the lunar sphere.

But the utterly absurd aspect about all this by-election fever is that the only people who are even remotely feverish ARE the media folk. The media folk love by-elections because there is always a chance of what they themselves call 'an upset'; that is to say at by-elections voters cast their ballots for all sorts of strange candidates rather than for all sorts of strange parties. There have been some very tasty by-election upsets too. Eric Lubbock's remarkable turn round in Orpington and Kent, Shirley Williams in Crosby, the disgraceful Peter Griffiths in Smethwick. Closer to home there has been Winnie Ewing in Hamilton and, of course, Margot in Govan itself. But not a single one meant anything. Despite what pundits say about blows to the defeated parties, by-elections lead on to nothing. The only by-elections which ever gave a clue were Kevin MacNamara's success at Kingston upon Hull, which led Harold Wilson to go to the country and win by a landslide, and perhaps the so-called Appeasement by-election just before the War when Quinton Hogg made his first appearance on the political stage. The rest are frothy, bubbly, but delicious little morsels for the press and TV. And the exxes would choke you chaps in Govan.

Staying at My Club

'I WAS walking somewhat in a muse when who should I
bump into but Sandy Arbuthnot, right at the steps of my
club.' Richard Hannay was always saying that in John
Buchan's stirring tales. Buchan was a great man for clubs.
So was Dornford Yates. Chesterton, both the Waughs,
Compton Mackenzie, R.L. Stevenson – the list could go on
forever – were great clubmen. Literary chaps being
members of clubs doesn't seem quite right somehow: you
expect a bit more boheme about them. There is nothing at
all Bohemian about your Urban Voltaire here. I am
becoming positively Establishment which is why, like any
other gentleman, I stay at my club when I go down to
Lond... I beg your pardon, when I go Up To Town.

Travelling down to the Great Wen recently I was forced to
share my first class (what else?) compartment with several
Celtic fans down to see the Arsenal game. It could have
been worse. They could have been Arsenal supporters up to
see the Bhoys.

The air was thick with cans of lager when one of lads
asked me how long I was down for. 'Where are ye steyin'?'
he then politely enquired. I had waited years for this. With
total relish I told him I was staying at my club. The lads
were intrigued. They had never heard of anyone staying at
a club. Clearly they envisaged a wee doss down beside the
Space Invader machine; or a bed made up on top of the pool
table. All they wanted to know was if you get a drink after
hours if you stayed in such a place. 'The block at the Rolls
Royce has ye oot at quarter past,' said one fan bitterly.

But it was none of your 'Time, gentlemen, please! Do your
talking while your walking while your talking!' stuff for me.
None of your bingo and darts rubbish. I was off to greater
things than that: off to penetrate the very bastions of the
British establishment.

I had had visions of dark-panelled rooms, heavy
deep-portraits of august figures of the past, the Times, The

71

Spectator, Horse and Hounds, lying discretely on the
morning-room table, kedgeree at breakfast time, faithful old
retainers greeting you at the door, crusted port to go with
the crusted members.

My club is the Savile, in Brook Street. The Savile has
dark-pannelled rooms, heavy deep-padded leather
armchairs, dim portraits of august figures of the past, all
the papers mentioned above, kedgeree for brekkers, and a
faithful old retainer in the shape of Cedric the barman. He
sold me a crusted port. Later at night I was to discover that
the members did indeed get crusted and in fact some of
them were crusted out of their skulls by the end of the
night. The club is quite clear on this matter. 'A gentleman is
expected to get drunk every now and again' a previous club
secretary is reported as saying. 'No gentleman would point
out a member's inebriation.' Most gentlemen's clubs have a
similar position.

Mind you there are occasions when a clubman fails to
behave like a gentleman. The Savile apparently once put
out a distinguished contributor to this very blatt, for
fighting in the lavatories with a Welsh Member of
Parliament. The reason why the chaps at the Savile
remembered the incident was that they felt sorry for the
scribe and said the Welsh MP had had it coming for years.

The Savile was everything I imagined it to be. The bar
was dark and inviting. So were the members. As the Savile
was started up as a convivial talking shop – its motto is
Sodalitas Convivium – there are demands made upon the
members to be especially welcoming to an out-of-town chap.
At one point I was talking to a strangely familiar fellow
with a dafter cover up hairstyle than my own. I realised
with a shock that it was Robert Robinson. I've heard him on
the airwaves so long it was like speaking to a wireless set.

If talking to other members is obligatory – for instance
you are not permitted to read in the bar or the dayroom – at

breakfast it is not. To intimate your desire not to be spoken
to you simply hoist your copy of a top people's blatt onto a
little stand provided for the purpose, and a very
gentlemanly notion that is too.

Breakfast incidentally is superb. Bloaters for Brekkers
was one of them. The actual dining room is magnificent –
with great marble and porphyry pillars and vast gilded
mirrors. The ballroom next door was even more superb and
was oddly feminine in its elegance. My favourite room
though was the library. A wonderfully apt note was
contained there: on the mantelpiece was a bust of, believe it
or not, Voltaire.

But your own Voltaire here was not going to spend all his
days in the one establishment and by no means. I was off to
the other London clubs for which I have reciprocity and the
next stop was the Garrick. The Garrick of course is the
thespians' club, started way back in 1831 in honour of the
great theatrical. It too is dark and wood-panelled and is so
ancient it looks a little like an old ship.

One of the members in here had sailed a little too close to
the wind too because he fell gracefully off his bar stool. I
was shocked at this but the barman wasn't and helpfully
guided the chap to a chair next door. Another nice touch: he
brought him a large whisky and soda.

The Savage club was awful – big, painted a sickly pale
green, with modern furniture and formica table tops. They
made me wear a tie in there. I suspect they wished I could
do something about my accent too, but probably consoled
themselves with the thought of Sir Billy Connolly who is
now clearly an aristocrat. The baleful influence of the lady
members was much in evidence. Nobody was drunk: but
then, nobody was talking to each other.

The Chelsea Arts Club was, as you would have expected,
very arty indeed and refreshingly different from all the

others I visited. It is fresh and open with enormous windows looking out onto a leafy garden. Inside the members wore jeans and open-necked shirts with bright bandanas at their throats. I started talking to a bloke who looked like Acker Bilk, and another fellow who wore a sombrero and an Inverness cape. He would have passed for one of the Wombles. He told me in a heavy Yorkshire accent that London was full of absolute bastards. The worst, he said, were the Scotch bastards.

It was clearly necessary for a wee investigation on my part as to the veracity of this statement. The obvious place to find this out was our own editor's London club, the Caledonian. This is going to upset the poor fellow but, truth to tell, I would as soon be put up at the Great bloody Eastern than doss down in this joint.

Needless to say we encountered one of these chaps who are always telling that they are 'proud to be a Scot' and tell you in an accent that makes Prince Charles sound like a scruff. He insisted on buying large Macallan malts all round. In the condition he was in he'd have been as well drinking Brasso himself, but then, a free half is not to be sniffed at.

But though I have visited more clubs – and I have more tales to tell of them – it was the Savile I took to most. Late at night, fiddling at the door with a silly little key and then inside to the empty bar to get at the night tray of whisky and gin and sherry, it was then I liked it best. I sat in the deep leather chair and sipped a night-cap and looked around the gleaming panelled walls and thought of all the ghosts who were doubtless fluttering unseen in this very room.

Here had been John Buchan and Dornford Yates once, talking in low whispers of the state of the Empire. Here Evelyn Waugh had insulted every member of the club and had stormed out apologetically. Chesterton had warmed his expansive rear at the fireplace across the way. R.L. Stevenson had told his stories of dark murders in Highland glens. Members all. And now they were joined by a wee Glaswegian yob like myself.

It was three in the morning. I sat in the quiet gloom of the Savile Club sipping a whisky as a sort of triumph came over me.

Bloody Heedrum Hodrums

SOONER OR LATER you are going to be sitting in front of that great computerised fireside they call the cathode ray tube and sooner or later you will find yourself switching on great swathes of rubbish which will then invite themselves into what was once your home. 'Crossroads' will distort Real Life, and 'The Winds of War' will have nothing to do with it, and the News will be from another planet altogether, and you will be assailed entirely with the saga of the Acquisitive Society and it is a lot worse if you have weans because they will hit you with 'The World of Television' quicker than a Metropolitan polis will fire pointy lead things into your mini and maybe quicker. And then, on that box, you will be brought down by a quick burst of Scottish Heritage.

It might well be a half-hour of the Fiddlers Rally (which has, of course, nothing to do with the goings on at your local government headquarters), and if the thought crosses your mind that we fought two world wars for the freedom to inflict this upon ourselves, this is as nothing to the angst produced by the notion that we are free to assault our nation with the broadcasting of The Mod.

Curious, isn't it, that this appalling jamboree should be called The Mod when it is as mod as a Sunday in Tiree, and curiouser still that it should be on the box and that responsible newspapers like This Great Rag should report any of this Heilan' Mince.

Switch on the telly during the mod and a young woman in

a tartan skirt, buck teeth, and a 1958 hairdo will be standing in front of a 1958 cameraman singing like your Aunty Bella did in 1958, only in Gaelic and getting a medal for it instead of a boot up her Heilan' jacksie. Worse is to come. Wee girls will appear, in kilts and starched white blouses, standing still in a Respect-for-Adults pose and chant shrilly in a language foreign to almost all of the five million inhabitants of Scotland who are, incidentally, at that moment missing the star movie that is being shown everywhere else in the UK.

This performance will be interrupted by another young woman whirling the Gaelic round her buck teeth. As the Gaelic sounds like a drunk being sick outside of a Byres Road pub but making a meal of it, one wonders why buck-teethed young women don't at least speak to us in a manner that could be understood. But Miss Buck Teeth is merely introducing us to another Heilan' Horror and in front of your unbelieving eyes will be a parade of 12 wee lassies with Scottish pudding faces operating three inoperable spinning wheels and slapping tweed between them while intoning heedrum hodrums, thereby displaying our Highland Heritage. There will be a bale of hay behind them as a stage prop, though the hay will be more realistic than the wee girls and their heedrum hodrums.

All of this is a stage prop, though, and as a piece of National Heritage it is as heritageous as the famed Glasgow Jeely Piece. It is all a cod.

By the way, the heritage of 12,000 people of the city of Glasgow is mainly Polish and Lithuanian, and 15,000 Glaswegians are of Italian origin and a lot of us are slightly Jewish and half the city is once from the peasant lands of Donegal and even Column Brogan is such a man who hails from there, but we are all as well getting the odd injection of our tartan heritage from time to time and give Moira Anderson and her pals a job of work to do. As it happens, my own ancestry is somewhat Highland, though my Grandpapa and Grandmama shot the craw from Mull pretty early on. The Grandpapa managed to croak it in the service of the Empire at Gallipoli, actually. A far cry that: from the lapping waters of Tobermory to the beaches of Gallipoli and away from the distillation of Highland Heritage.

But I am not having the Highland Heritage. I am not having the Gaelic Lobby and their ersatz culture, their language and ideology, their notion that poverty is all the different for being spoken in Gaelic rather than English. By God, these same teuchters were pulling forelocks to the Laird while my grandma was in service and in service to the Manse at that: the Highland Heritage at its most pusillanimous.

While the Gaelic Lobby and the Highland Heritagers were talking inconsequences up in their but and bens there were the same Gaels down in the shipyards, and the factories and steelworks, and in the dark satanic mills. Damn all good was Highland Heritage to those men and women huddled in the dark tenements of Glasgow. For eighty years or more Glasgow, this city, and the grim towns around it, has fuelled the economy of this land, has fed the nation, and damn the thanks they were given from as mean-spirited and small-minded a nation of ingrates as you will find on this earth – from the Scots outside of the dreadfully scarred industrial belt of the West.

And as a reward for the toil and work, the only real life left in this northern land, you will get the ravings of nationalists and the bleating of a well-fed Gaelic breast. And sooner or later, in front of your TV set, you will get the final insult: the faint smell of virtue from the fantasists with their 12 wee girls in kilts and starched blouses, from the heedrum hodrums. The faint smell of virtue, and of jealousy, death and decay.

Women

The Battle of the Sexes

WOMEN ARE frequently ridiculous creatures. I can't think why: it must just be the way their mums bring them up. Of course, males are frequently ridiculous too – just think of Mussolini or Hitler or Cecil Parkinson. But men are ridiculous in a sort of weak way, all pomposity and poor-mouthing. Women are frequently silly in an unknowing way. The reason why, for instance, a hen-pecked man is such a figure of fun is because a nagging wife is even more such. I am not saying that men aren't ludicrous, or that the notion of male wisdom and gravitas at all times isn't just the same. I am saying that it does not do to ascribe stupidity to the male sex alone. And it is not on to insist on omniscience to the lassies.

Here is some drivel: 'Women do grow up, whereas men stay boys'. It comes from the mouth of the photogenic Emma Sergeant, a high profile Society bint who plays with paint on the side. She was one of the female luminaries but recently quoted in a Top People's paper in England. The comments of herself and her fellow distaff celebs were dreadfully revealing, my dears. Shirley Conran, (novelist, the paper describes her), said that men were more badly indoctrinated than women. She said, pithily, that she would quite like to be brought up as a man 'brought up by me' she said. Well she's got a son brought up by her – called, predictably, Jasper – and he looks a shocking wimp and designs clothes which only a rich and neurotic dyslexic who fell off her horse at a too early age could be expected to don.

Another of the female of the species, a Ms. Sonia Melchett, (author, hostess, whatever that is), said that women were clearer-headed, (though surely more grammatical), than men. She also claimed to have sat on the board of the NSPCC and been a magistrate. Being a hostess, like, must have been a right qualification for being a magistrate. There are times when the upper classes make you want to be violently ill.

But there were more in this Top People's paper bizarre survey. Besides a novelist and a hostess, (whatever that is), there were another novelist, a doctor and Dame of the British Empire, a critic, five actresses, two editors, two TV personalities, several businesswomen, and two peeresses.

There was, as well, a headmistress of an expensive girl's school, a film producer, an alleged broadcaster, a ballerina, and Miss Koo Stark, described as a photographer. That is a turn up, as they say, for the books, Miss Stark being mainly noted for being on the other side of the camera, for being well-named, and for jouking about with one of the Royal wimps. It is indeed a motley crew: on with the motley.

As it happens, most of the ladies concerned said, or wrote I suppose, very sensible things in the main. Olivia de Havilland stated clearly that she didn't pay much attention to women or what they have to say. Didn't have much respect for women's minds. 'They are appallingly inaccurate, superficial,' and according to this clear-thinking lady, 'lacked judgement'. I don't know who edits what seems to be the woman's page of this English Top People's Paper, but if I was a woman I would be howling for her instant dismissal. Not because she allowed old Olivia de Havilland to say the most outrageous things, no matter how true, about the female sex, but because it surely doesn't matter what a collection of old boots – with the exception of the delectable Miss Stark – who are positively FILTHY with money and/or Establishment prestige, I say, it simply doesn't count a damn what they have got to speak of about men and women and the difference between them and whether men are more ridiculous than women or the other way round. I will tell you this about women.

I will tell you this: for far too long you women out there have allowed such travesties as 'Women's' magazines and 'Women's' page and 'Women's' bloody Hour, and 'Women's' interests. There are undoubtedly cultural areas which belong to either sex and such items should be catered for, even on Top People's blatts. I would simply ignore such bits, as I do the stuff on golf, or murders, or, hill-walking. 'Women's stuff' should be there without nomenclature because Humanity is roughly split between both sexes and what mainly concerns blokes mainly concerns birds. Here is a thing which mainly concerns both lots. That blatts and telly progs and all the rest of the circus are forever giving you out a load of old cobblers about what rich and successful people, with damn-all to do with the majority of normal people, think about any bloody spurious idea other rich and successful people can come up with over an amusing dinner party in Chelsea and shove into the blatt owned by their own kind.

As it happens, I haven't the slightest scooby about women's minds myself and I am not interested in finding out either considering the outcome of past attempts to do so. I know that it is as silly to go about imagining the womenfolk to be frothy little things without an idea in their heads except frocks as it is for the women to think of men as 'really little boys at heart.' For a start I have seen some little boys at heart who would make the blood run cold even with the courage of a drink in you.

I have seen hard-working women and wives and mothers struggling against the tide of life and their husbands, weary with effort, and all the punditry of actresses and novelists and other fashionables, regardless of their sex, is bloody meaningless to them. The Top People's blatts are, of course, an insult to us all, as all the utter drivia, (good word that, just thought it up), that you will find in the fashion pages and the Sunday Supps, and the nonsense on the telly and the radio are damned contumelies to the poor, the old, and all the rest we socialist chaps are forever invoking. But even the fashionables can be sensible. One of the famous names was quoted in the article of which I speak. Said Margharita

Laski: 'My hands are better suited to fine needle-work, my husband's hands are better suited to carpentry.' Makes you think, that. My hands are suited to neither.

Foreign Birds

YOUNG CHAPS have fantasies: old chaps have fantasies. I sometimes imagine the ceremony for my Pulitzer Prize. Not many young fellows have dreams like that: they are far too bloody sensible. Young fellows confine their fantasies mostly to sexual ones. I have them too but they are shadowy cobwebs now and – if you will excuse me – just as gossamer thin at that. The younger blokes eroticism of their dreams seems to them to have the potentiality – indeed the potency – of substance. One of the biggest fantasies of all is foreign birds.

There was a time in my youth when I could not get foreign birds off the brain: it was the movies mostly. While all the girls of my acquaintance and all those of my chums possessed a frustrating chasteness, the foreign birds in all the movies were raving nymphomaniacs. It didn't seem fair, being British. Thus it is that vast hordes of youths escape to foreign climes determined to sow themselves at will. I know all about this AIDS thing. When you are nineteen though you will brave castration just for a bit of the other and all the scarifying telly ads in the world will not put an end to the bridling carnality of Youth. AIDS frightens the hell out of me, but then I am now of an age when everything else – including women – does that already. It is all very well telling young men to take our advice and go celibate or blind or something; young men will not take it. When it comes to foreign birds you would be as well talking to a canary. But for what my advice is worth here it is.

Do not be misled by movies. Foreign birds are by no means nymphomaniacs. In fact, foreign girls are not even romantic. It is this island race who are romantic. There are no Latin people as soppy about their womenfolk as to go around habitually addressing them as 'Love', 'Darling', 'Sweetheart', or even the Glaswegian 'Hen'. The foreigners are bloody to their women. Their women are worse, to their men.

Take the Frogs. If French men are venal, ill-mannered, vain, and unhygienic they have probably learnt it all at their mothers' knees. Frenchwomen fall into three basic categories. They are either under-age coquettes in the Brigitte Bardot mould, or they are femme fatales in the Jeanne Moreau style. Or they are concierges, thin with sharp lips and dressed in funereal black. You will find the latter category of Frenchwomen much in the majority. This is because even the nymphette and the most sophisticated of Parisiennes will eventually end up as the concierge type.

Frenchwomen have undeniable wiles to get round men and this can blind the innocent, well, Abroad, if you like. Frenchwomen by tradition do not shave under their armpits and as they are a somewhat hirsute lot one regularly notes that the Gaelic female seems to be wearing a sporran in each oxter. It is a touch off-putting, though not nearly as bad as the Don Ameche moustache which the average French girl sports. You will discover too that the French are an uncleanly race and that their women smell of old bra straps. There is a reason for this. You should see their bras.

Another intriguing fact about French females is that they never, ever, go to the lavatory. If you have seen the state of French plumbing you will understand why. This however leads to constant moaning about liver problems. Your problem as a young chap is worse than theirs with their bladders. French girls require a heavy expenditure and the age of consent is nineteen. My advice to you is to leave French girls to French boys. They don't do any better with their womenfolk but the French male is due it anyway. Incidentally, the Belgian bints are fatter Frenchwomen who wear corsets and knit lace. You should see the German madchen.

German girls are big and blonde and blonde and big. If they are not that they are thin-lipped and dark and belong to the Baader-Meinhof Gang. The blondes of Bavaria are especially typical of German womanhood. Even as little girls, no matter how pretty, they have the very look upon them which allows you to envisage them as they will be like when they are their mothers age. The southern Germans affect Drindl. which can be very attractive, as can their blonde locks tied primly into plaits. There is something wonderfully repressive about their appearance. German women are just not repressive about themselves however: they are particularly repressive about their men. This is probably why the Germans of yesteryear went about giving each other duelling scars and cavorting about in silly uniforms. Only the Germans could ever have felt serious in jodhpurs and black shirts. Another point: German women can't cook.

If you particularly vomit at the aftertaste of sauerkraut and Blutwurst, you will starve in Spain where the food is cooked in axle-grease. The Spanish hausfrau cooks badly and dresses worse. She is bizarrely pious. It is difficult to envisage Spanish women ending up this way because they start well. Spanish girls are − I was going to say impenetrable but this sounds a little recherche to be honest. Spanish girls go everywhere with chaperones even in the freedom of the cities. Spanish girls are cruel, but then they have to be considering the fiends that represent Spanish manhood. Spanish girls despise British men, finding them lacking in machismo. Carmen was Spanish. Look what happened to Jose.

Italian women, like Italian blokes, are at first sight much the best of a bad bunch on the continent of Europe. The young signorine are astonishingly pretty, dark-haired, dark-lashed, olive-skinned, sensual and voluptuous and with a disarming innocence. I have been in love with Italian girls ever since I first clapped eyes on Giglio Cincquetta not to mention Gina Lollabrigida. They make most attractive middle-aged wives too, fat and jolly and wonderful cooks. The problem is that they make this metamorphosis from girl to fat housewife about the age of twenty-two.

Greek women are halfway between Latins and Levantines. If you wondered at the thin moustaches of the French maids you should see the upper lips of Greek lassies. The would put Jimmy Edwards to shame. Greek women are very dram-a-tic and Melina Mercouri should put you off them for life.

At first sight Scandinavian women appear extremely desirable. They are blonde and cool and altogether ice-maidens unless they are called Britt Ekland. They are also held to be sexually liberated and pro-free love. In actuality they are not to be held at all because they are nearly as boring as Scandinavian men which is to say that they can bore in eight languages. Most Scandinavian men commit suicide just to get some peace.

But there are all sorts of girls abounding on the continent. Dutch girls are plump and have minds made out of glass. Swiss maids are strictly for the Swiss and will talk to nobody less than a hotelier if not a banker – I said banker. The hordes of American females wandering about Yurrup on daddy's money are impossible. American women have mouths so big that they look as if they are eating themselves when they talk. Arab women are either swaddled in their chador or their men will carve you up on the spot for a stray glance.

Your best bet is with the British lassies, though I am bound to tell you that most of them can consume a very expensive bottle of vodka no bother costing you a fortune before they tell you to push off at the end of the night. Scots girls will hit you with the empty and knee you in the groin as their version of a goodnight kiss. It is no fun at all.

But it does not matter what I tell you young chaps out there. You will be spending your nights – and your money – hunting for the female of the species, desperate for a bite at the forbidden fruit. It does not matter when I tell you of the of the frustration of it all, or of the grief you are bound to come to, or of the fact that because of your fruitless pursuit you will be going home with your pockets full of fingers and damn-all else. I know you will not listen.

But bear this in mind as you throw yourselves on the holiday resort this summer. I have spoken with the wisdom of the ages but I am not so wise myself. I too can be deluded by the shadow of an eyelash upon a blooming cheek. And the sibilant swish of a dress across a creamy thigh. I could go on like this. I am no wiser than the young. The difference is that I have less chance of any kind of success at all.

Lock Up Your Daughters
'I LOATHE ABROAD... and as for foreigners, they are all the same and they all make me sick.' Nancy Mitford wrote with her usual calm, measured logic. Mind you, she wrote that back in 1945 when foreigners were probably pretty grim at that. Of course young English ladies were of the opinion that everybody was a foreigner unless they had been at school with them or their brothers. Upper class fellows were convinced that the lower orders smelled and might as well be damned Frogs or Onion Johnnies anyway.

It seems that few young ladies share Ms. Mitford's opinion these days. The average British maiden thinks of practically nothing else all year but going off to some appalling Mediterranean high rise slum and spending all day getting sunburn on a stretch of bleak sand, and last but by no means least meeting some foreign chap. Very keen on foreign chaps, British maidens are. Think they have glamour.

It's the TV and the movies which gives the girls that impression. The hard reality of a first holiday abroad will soon dislodge that. A gruesome lot foreigners are, I can tell you. Many's the young girl who has spent her hard-earned holiday abroad in tears upon making this discovery. It is for the benefit of young maidens in this island everywhere that I therefore will blow the whistle on our continental cousins. Believe me girls, you will be thanking your Uncle Jack here before your first twenty-four hours in foreign climes is out.

The first thing you have to know is that foreigners not only do not have the lingo, they do not have the manners either. The Northern Europeans think all girls are theirs for the asking, and the Southern Europeans don't even ask. The Latins are so keen on locking up their own girls that they positively pounce on British females. Given half a chance they will ponce on them as well, for their rigid morality only extends to their own daughters and sisters. As for those Europeans at the edge of the Middle East, a large number of those chaps possess somewhat Arab proclivities and will not bother lassies at all.

There are young ladies around who yet believe that European men are romantic, exotic, and handsome. Let me disabuse them of this notion. Look at our nearest neighbours, the French.

The French male is vain: not in the childish naive way that the Italian is, but vain in an all-round egocentric way. He thinks of himself as a connoisseur of fine wines and food; as a bon vivant and boulevardier; even as something of a philosopher. In reality the Frenchman is obsessed with his digestion, especially his foie, is surly and morose, and his philosophical powers extend to merely thinking of all times of himself. He exults in rodomontade. Hazlitt got it right when he claimed that it was 'vanity driven from all other shifts, and forced to appeal to itself for admiration.' Nobody admires the French more than the French. Furthermore, the French male is a peculiarly nasty looking bit of work. Just look at the swarthy pock-marked complexion, the beaky nose, the way the eyebrows meet in the middle. Note especially the sneer on the upper lip. It is clear to me that the French sneer came first, and the accent naturally followed, directed by the twisted shape of the lips. I need say nothing about the Garlic-and-Gitane induced effluvia from the French male breath. His laundry leaves a lot to be desired. He himself is not to be desired at all.

Do not bother about the Belgians. They are just shorter, fatter Frenchmen who eat chips with everything.

Let us now turn our attention to the bold hidalgos of Spain. A cruel looking people Spaniards are: they have faces like hawks. Note the thin hard lips and the high cheekbones like razors. When the Spaniard smiles, which he does chillingly, he reveals a mouthful of gold molars. The hair is thick and greasy. But not as greasy as he is. His behaviour towards women is atrocious, and consists of keeping Spanish girls in virginal prisons until they marry when they turn into black-garbed drudges. The word 'machismo' is of course Spanish. A wee squint inside a Madrid cafe will soon show you what they mean by it.

The Italians are Latins too, at first sight a more attractive set of chaps. The word for them is 'braggadocio'. Italian men are fond of posing as imposing and Mussolini could have been of no other country. They have, as the poet hath it 'an itch for the praise of fools.' The Italian male loves dressing up, and he loves dressing down – it was the Italians who invented the shirt open to the waist and a wall of gold geegaws erected upon his manly hairy chest. An Italian man's idea of a love affair is five minutes in bed and the rest of the night telling his pals about it. Greeks, incidentally, are Italians who only shave once a week.

Now we come to the Germans. There are two types of German males. One is tall, blond, with piercing blue eyes.

He is the stuff of which Nazi legend was made and is always the type who plays a Panzer tank commander in the movies. He is well outweighed by the other class of German male. Most Germans are short and squat and very, very greedy when it comes to grub. They like to drink out of silly jugs and sing loud marching songs and the Southern ones wear dafter clothes than even the moderator of the Church of Scotland dons which is really saying quite a lot. Many young Germans do not look like this stereotype at all of course, but they will, my dears, in the fullness of time, they will.

All Scandinavians, except the Norwegians, are pleasant fellows, and often handsome fellows too. However as Scandinavian ladies are well liberated you will find that Scandinavian desire is not of the romantic variety and they are in Europe simply to escape from the awful bloody boredom of their own countries. My singling out of Norwegians (above) may seem somewhat enigmatic. I knew several Norwegian students when I was at Art College those many years ago and found them an arrogant lot. Quisling came from Norway.

But you will discover men of many races on your holiday abroad, and I tell you, you will not be impressed. The Dutch all smoke dope, the Portuguese eat fish all the time. From further afield, the Japanese tourists which abound throughout Europe only have eyes for their own womenfolk or for a camera viewfinder. The Australians are boorish and drunken, (and sneer even better than the French). The few Americans who weren't too feart of coming to Europe are too feart of AIDS to press any kind of suit whatsoever. The English males all either come from Bradford or Doncaster and are simply out of the question. There is one last important race of men.

These males are short and bow-legged. They are foul-mouthed and alcoholic. Their evening wear consists of a slept-in tee shirt, a pair of jeans in tatters, with tell tale marks which signify public urination, and training shoes which have been boiled in chip fat. They are generally a low-browed race and their speech, which is coarsely accented, fashions no philosophy save that pertaining to drink or football. They leer more horribly than any spick, dago, wop, frog or fritz. And the irony for you girls out there is that it was exactly this race of ignoble savages that you went away to escape from in the first place.

Nancy Mitford also said that she thought Abroad utterably bloody, adding that 'foreigners are fiends.' But to any decent young girl I should have thought all men were a foreign country.

Thoughts of Youth

Discipline of the Mind

'HOW DARE YOU?' wrote a reader about my column a while back when I castigated the existence of weans. She went on to suggest that the source of my malevolence towards the creatures was envy at their 'exuberance and vitality,' stating that I had none of the above qualities left in myself. I deny that aspersion. When it comes to my dislike of children I'm practically Sammy Davis Junior in my exuberance and vitality. The only time you will see a flicker of vigour in myself is when you mention the word 'wean' to me. I loath the things with a deep and devout fervour.

I may say that my misanthropy has been vindicated by none other than the Princess Royal who confessed the other week that she couldn't stick the diminutive homunculi, even though out of the sort of regal decency which we have come to expect from the Windsors she still thinks we should do the right thing by the brats. Princess Anne can't bear a brat either, but it doesn't stop her from working damned hard for the Save the Children Fund.

I reiterate for the benefit of my irate correspondent: I would rather have cockroaches in my house than children – but I still believe that they are entitled to a decent education.

Here is another vindication of myself. It was but a few months back that I obtained the sort of opprobrium normally reserved for the Ku Klux Klan from primary schoolteachers as a result of an article I wrote about their craft. They especially objected to my phrase about their 'placenta-pink sentimentality.'

Offensive as the very phrase seems to have been, it was as nothing to the offence I apparently gave to the poor lassies (some of them are chaps, I am told, but it still seems a lassies' job to me) because I questioned the ideology that underlies their practice. I'm by no means the first to do so, as it happens, but as the majority of primary teachers haven't read a book without pictures or one that didn't bounce off a college of education list I'm unsurprised at their ignorance.

Wrote that doyen of columnists, the late Henry Mencken: 'I suggest hanging all the professors of pedagogy, arming the ma'am with a rattan and turning her loose.'

Mencken wrote this over half-a-century ago and true it is today. But not only was he correct; so was I. For if Princess Anne has vindicated my thesis about weans, recent research has proved that placenta-pink sentimentality gibe of mine to be right with a red tick and a vg at the bottom of the page.

For it has now emerged that the standard of arithmetic is lower among Scottish children than it was even a few years ago. The Education Minister, Michael Forsyth, was – and is – right to be very concerned about this. Yet it is small wonder.

For primary schools are awash with nonsense. The primary teachers – mostly soft-centered women admittedly – are running about like hens without heids trying to produce a curriculum for the little beasts which will interest them; and bear in mind that the individual child comes first in the Alice-in-Wonderland world of the primary school, which will produce a wall full of brightly coloured mince that satisfies fond parents, education officials, school inspectors, and visiting councillors, instead of trying for a roomful of interior knowledge in the wean's head.

I have said it before and in the time-honoured way I will say it again. By the time children get to a real education in a secondary school, they've had so little of the basic discipline by which you actually LEARN that they might as well go straight into whatever modern version we have of putting bits of boys and girls up chimneys.

I know the primary teachers don't believe this. They wouldn't, would they? Brainwashed as the poor things are by the (mainly) male teachers at their colleges of education, where they went in the first place because they couldn't get into a yooni, the primary teachers have come to have faith in a system designed to exhaust them and neuroticise children into a never-ending demand for meaningless enjoyment.

Of course the children can't read anymore, and the few who do read salivating drivel anyway. Of course they can't write a proper hand. More of them write with an aerosol spray than with a fountain pen. Of course they can't count: they have calculators bought by star-struck parents. None of them knows a foreign language, and Latin and Greek are now being touted as fun rather than what the study of them is for. The discipline of the mind. Aye, there's the rub.

The discipline of the mind now: that's a hard one. The Government doesn't like the sound of that – it might lead to the independence of it and that would never do. The radicals don't like it because it reminds them of the dark days when children were told what to do. The careerists in modern-day teaching don't admire such a concept either, because they have no discipline themselves and are shamed by those who possess such a thing.

I'm going to get a lot more letters from primary teachers and the like over this one. 'How dare you?' they will all start. I dare to. I doubly dare to, and more.

Opportunity Makes a Thief

I ONCE stole out of a shop: I was twelve. I embarked upon this life of crime by pinching a bar of McCowan's Highland Toffee. It was the cheap bar, not even the one with chocolate. Sadly my career as a top thief was nipped in the bud because I was caught by the shopkeeper. Being an amateur in the theft business, I chose the shop across the road from our house where my Da got his fags from every morning and, to cut a long story short, the owner told my Da, and the resulting interview with my shamed and irate parent delivered to myself a quite rigourous respect for the consequences of larceny or any other crime against society if it comes to that. To this day I would find it impossible to steal anything just in case my dad might come down from Valhalla and give me a similar doing to the one I got when I tried to steal a bar of awful toffee. I don't steal and I despise those who do.

But I get stolen from: a lot. Just before Christmas I had my house burgled. Truth to tell, they didn't take very much really. They pissed over my bed and they defecated on the hall carpet and they caused a lot of damage to the front door and they ripped out the telephone. The polis told me that the youths who turned me over were nervous and the incontinence is the result of their little anxieties. They took the video and a couple of boxes of irreplaceable records and my late mother's wedding and engagement rings. The last were quite worthless because dad hadn't very much money in 1940 and my mum had worn the things till they were cobweb thin. Oddly enough, I was annoyed but not insane with anger. Ever more oddly, I hadn't any insurance at all because I am incompetent in my private life to a degree which probably suggests being put away for my own good.

But, after all, I am used to being stolen from. In schools I have had damn-near everything I have possessed stolen from me. I have had two lovely gold pens whipped. It was suggested that I should not have brought such luxuries into educational establishments in the first place, or have left my jacket lying or, anyway, been able to possess such symbols of sybarity in the first place. It is all my fault really. I have had packets of fags pinched out of desk drawers, ten pound notes from coat pockets, cigarette lighters, scarves, pairs of leather gloves: once, even, a painting I had committed for use in my club. God knows what lumpen Toryglen family possesses a McLean original. Strewth, I hadn't even signed it.

Then they stole my hat. Fifty quid's worth of hat. They stole it from a decent little boozer in the West End of Glasgow. A nice wee pub with nice people in it and not a body in sight you could think of who would ever do such a thing as steal from anybody else. It wasn't like the burglary. The young villains who had, as they say, tanned my house, didn't have a clue about who they were stealing from, who they were violating. They'd never met me. In the house quick, adrenalin racing through their veins, get the video, a couple of cheap rings, the passport, and off. Piss on his bed. Crap on the floor. They didn't know me. The characters who stole my hat saw me standing at the bar, and their victim was flesh and blood and the sort of bloke you would find standing in any pub except maybe for the hat. I will tell you that the likely possibility is that they even recognised me as the wee minor celeb... with the hat. So they stole it. A taxi driver told me later that he saw it drifting across the New City Road, being driven over by every passing car. It was a lovely hat.

It was a lovely hat and part of me and my projected persona I suppose. It had a wide brim, straight out of the movies, and the inside of it looked as resplendent as a new box of cutlery for a bride. I bought it and wore it with a certain uncertainty in this city because, after all, this is the city in which the punters are ever ready to discover a pretension or a vanity. I put up with the burglary, just as I have put up with the theft of pens and packets of B & H and all the rest of it. If some of you have thought that I've gone right-wing recently, listen to this. If I ever find out who stole my hat he will limp for the rest of his life. Worse, I would bring the birch back and, dammit, I'd do it myself.

Because it isn't just the hat: it's everything. I have had the lack of a moral bloody structure in this society up to here. I am sick of the lawlessness which urban society in particular accepts as its due. It is all very well for middle-class people – Tory or Labour voting – to sit in the Olympian heights and say that trouble should be dealt with by the police. I will tell you: I am, unfortunately, like so many of us out there, too close to the sad and alienated population who steal and destroy and neglect their kids and beat their wives and get ludicrously and aggressively drunk and . . . I am too close to that for comfort.

I have spent too long getting baited by children with the I.Q.'s and the moralities of rats for no reason other than that I'm a nice enough fellow with an education. Bullied by the kind of lumpen terrorism that, as a Glaswegian, I have had to live with for far too long. And stolen from at every opportunity by people who can eventually be lionised by the Edinburgh New Town bourgeoisie. I am heartily sick of it.

Here is a vision. One day the respectable working classes will be forced to discipline the lumpen because the middle classes won't do it for them. The housing schemes will have vigilanti and there will be the breath of Fascism across the land. I see apocalypse. In the meantime my hat blows with the wind across the wastelands.

Gymslips and Black Stockings

SCHOOLGIRLS. Delicious word. Goes with saucy. You can't deny that the word 'schoolgirls' is, well, delicious. It is not quite so delicious though if you happen to work in a school all the same. In fact, some schoolgirls have been among the most evil creatures I have ever met. I remember a whole class of them once, years ago, who engraved their names with terror upon my heart. Karen, Gail, Carol, Martha, Lisa, especially Lisa. Lisa was no mischievous pigtail-swinging little minx either: she was an utter bitch. She made Snow White's stepmother look like Cinderella. I saw her a few years ago on the street, literally, because it turned

95

out that her profession was walking it, and to my astonishment she was extremely pretty. It was then that I remembered with a touch more objectivity than I possessed back in the days when she reduced my daily life to misery. She had been astoundingly pretty then too. I'd never noticed. I only saw her appalling behaviour. I only saw her gargoyle of a soul. To me she had practically the head of a medusa.

Schoolgirls though. A very delicious word. One imagines demure young damsels in overtight blouses, straw hats, black stockings, especially black stockings. Oh, Mr. Edward Millar, Director of Education for Strathclyde has nothing to worry about me in this department. In the school I teach in the only use the brats would have for black stockings would be to use over the coupon for a bank job.

There is indeed the odd pretty wee girl in my school. The way I feel every day in my shop though I wouldn't notice Bo bloody Derek if she came in wearing nothing but a hat, straw or otherwise. Eddie Millar of Strathclyde Education Carnival can feel safe with me and my colleagues. In my place the merry little students drive you to such a condition that you don't need bromide in your tea. Your brain is so feverish just coping with the catering boys class that the rest of the body hasn't a look in. Every now and again you have to check to make sure that you're still intact and bits of you haven't atrophied in the last week and a half.

But schoolgirls. Delicious is the very word. I saw entire divisions of them in the city centre this week, just after four it was. There were hundreds of them. I counted. There were the ones in the imperial purple of Westbourne school for Young Ladies. There were young ladies too in the rich chocolate of Craigholme. Schoolgirls in St Aloysian green, other in the priggish raiment of Hutchesons Girls, those with the flash of the green collar of Park. It was a lecher's nightmare. The sight of them would have roused Malcolm

Muggeridge. I admit it, Dr. Millar of Strathclyde Education a week in one of those hothouses they call girls fee-paying schools and I would be in the jail.

How, you may reasonably be asking, and particularly reasonably if you have a young nymph of a daughter at such establishments as mentioned above, how do I recognise the schools by their blazers? I bet you suspect that I have made a wee hobby of spying schoolgirls on the street, probably the man probably knocks knickers off washing lines, you'll be thinking to yourself, I know the type HE is, I'll bet you'll be saying in heavy disapproval.

Ah, there is more than one explanation of my omniscience in the matter of schoolgirls uniforms, and I never nicked a knocker, er, knocked a knicker, in my life. The truth is, chaps, that I remember the hue of a blazer, the colour of a skirt, the shade of a gym slip sash from when I was just a lad. For, back in the early 'Sixties' I and lots of you fellows reading this in shocked voyeurism this very minute, used to go to the EL GUERO after school.

The El Guero was in the basement of the Ca'doror building and Reo Stakis owned it. It was the first self-service snack bar in Glasgow. For an hour after four it was infested with schoolgirls, in all shapes and sizes, in blue, brown, green, purple. They wore impossible hats impossibly pinned with kirbygrips at the back of their impossible heads. Their trench coats were clenched tightly round their slim waists by their belts, but not as tightly clenched as they would have been if I'd ever have got anywhere near them. They wore mascara and smoked elegantly. They talked conspiratorially with each other. Occasionally some extraordinarily handsome youth with yellow hair and looking like Tory Donahue who also played for Scottish Schoolboys and drove his own car red MG with spoke wheels was permitted to join these creatures.

We other schoolboys sat resentfully looking across at the femme fatales, trying to get our cigarette smoke to drift casually out of our nostrils at the same time as our mouths, furiously coughing. You sat, miserably, conscious of the ink stains on your fingers, of the fact that your attempt to take in your own trousers to a width which no normal foot could penetrate had resulted in what appeared to be jodhpurs, and jodhpurs soaked in chip fat at that. The spotty boys – I never had spots myself, at least not on the outside – went through faceburning agony each time a set of schoolgirl lashes lingered languidly for two seconds at the ravage of the acne on their beardless chins. Desire, lust, shame, awkwardness misery, you went through more emotions than a Taylor-Burton, marriage.

It all came back to me, this week in the city. The girl from St. Aloysius with the dark Italianate look of a Renaissance princess, gorgeously prim in her starched white collar and tie, the haughty blonde beauty with brown eyes from Westbourne: I caught the very edges of them this week, and was reduced to fifteen again, complete with ink stains and hot flushes. Delicious. Schoolgirls. But I can't go through all that again. Delicious is too much pain for raddled age to bear.

The Arts

I am an Artist

OH I AM all for Art: have made a sort of living out of it myself. Drawling and ratching and fainting by coils, Lewis Carroll called it. Greenery-yallery, said W.S. Gilbert. Seemed to suggest Art was some kind of dodge. So it is. I am, myself, a bit of a Philistine concerning Art, and a bit of an expert too, because I AM an artist and a chap who can draw a little. It happens that I have even become something of an Art Critic and those of you lucky enough to be recipients of that splendid cultural free-sheet, 'CULTURE CITY', will have discovered my expertise concerning the plastic arts which is to say the paintings, drawings, sculpture, photies, and all round onanism which celebrates itself in gallery after greenery-yallery gallery throughout this benighted little burg. I am your man for The Art.

I have witnessed the rise of young chaps straight out of art school and asking several large coarse G. notes for their scribblings. I have seen, with my own eyes, my dears, naked greed in the guise of London dealers' demands in a Glaswegian auction. The Big Bang has ensured that young wealthy chaps and chapettes have to find something to stick their poppy into, and a combination of wall-status and investment potential has created a boom in the Art business. Few of the young painters whose work is currently enjoying entrepreneurial success will last anyway. Apart from the utter spuriousness of the paintings concerned it happens that the young shavers had no expertise about the proper priming of their canvases and many of their paintings will slide off, tired and incompetent, in the next ten years anyway. Good luck to them.

It does not do, however, to be triumphalist about all of this. We critics should be assiduously agreeing with anything which makes mugs of the public especially if that public is well-heeled, as well as ignorant. The more ignorant you are about Art the more likely you are to be taken in anyway. The average working class fellow thinks art is a load of crap to begin with and is a most unlikely customer. If an artist REALLY wants to take the piss he looks for the sort of chap who unstintingly admires the Emperor's pink little body. He looks, in short, for a mug.

Now it happens that there are lots of mugs out there, but the biggest mugs are the ones who pay for daftness. They are called tax-payers. There are lots of ways in which the tax-paying mugs are taken for a ride and one of the methods is the one by which The Arts gets paid for. There is Opera and Ballet and symphonic music and theatre and, all in all, the Arts is magic when it comes to making a spondulick or two and is at least less risky than selling patent medicine at a huckster's stall. The visual arts is a stoatir.

In the old days it was quite hard really. You had to display a certain type of expertise, drawing properly, getting a likeness, making things look pretty: that sort of thing. It is changed days now. It would be a MOST unfortunate circumstance if one's work were to look like the thing portrayed: in such an unlikely case the young artist would simply bugger it up a touch. 'Gets to the quintessential nature underlying the... ' the critics will say. You should see what the THIRD EYE CENTRE is getting up to these days.

I don't know why it is called THE THIRD EYE CENTRE. They could call themselves the eighth testicle symposium with more reason as far as this raddled old cynic can see. It is an arts centre, whatever that is. It has a new thing on in it at the moment which it succinctly titles 'NEW WORK: NO DEFINITION'. I am not sure it has no definition, but the definition I would come up with has no place in what is bizarrely described as a family newspaper except to adumbrate that the definition is one word and starts with 'S' and ends with 'E' and has five letters and describes ordure with a working-class accent. Listen to this shite:

'IN NEW WORK/NO DEFINITION preconceptions of a theatre language are broken down. It is not theatre of the playwright but theatre of the visual artist.' According to the drivel put out by this absurd organisation this farrago seeks 'a new theatrical language as against the tyranny of the printed text'. We are told this piece of tendentious mince comes from a chap called Robert Dawson Scott, reviewing another chap (?) called Ralf Ralf in THE TIMES. I will bet they both Ralfed all the way to the Barclay's branch. Another critic spoke well of the venture. Her name is Naseem Khan. I am a bit surprised as this is the same name as a small girl I taught last year possesses. All I can say is that the wee lassie's English has not improved. Understandably Edinburgh's Traverse Theatre is inexplicably involved in this nonsense.

You should see what No Definitions has got marked out for you. There is a crew called KEITH McINTYRE AND ROTATING DANCERS SCOTLAND. The last time I saw rotating dancers I had been drinking heavily and a very arresting sight it was. There is an installation/performance concerning the diaries of a bint called Mona Hatoum, well, actually it is her dad's diaries about the war in Lebanon. I am simply GLAD that my taxes are paying for this. I am also impressed by something called 'DOGS IN HONEY'. This deals with 'sexuality in terms of strength, beauty and fear.' 'Images,' says the blurb, 'are drawn from science fiction, Brooklyn apartments, water, dirt, plastic and meal times'. Another riveting burst of art says we can enjoy 'images of sexuality, beauty and fear,' (I seem to have heard of this before), 'using images of glamour, Milton Keynes, cleanliness, architecture and ...'.

Later in this ludicrous programme I discovered the name of a young fellow with whom I was myself at Art College. He had then little talent. He is described in the most fulsome of terms. There is another work which is titled 'A VISION OF LOVE REVEALED IN SLEEP'. All of this is subsidised by the Scottish Arts Council. I suddenly feel tired and a little old and grey and full of sleep. I will hide my head amid a crowd of stars.

The Sons of the Desert

TONIGHT THE red fezzes will be out. The Crest Hotel in this city of Culture will be awash with them. There will be a buffet in the Pink Pup and lots of movies and it will all end up with a Sing-a-long in Fin's Soda Fountain Bar. You think that's bizarre? You should see the programme for tomorrow. That involves a fancy dress banquet followed by Earsey, Nosey, Kneesey and a stirring egg shelling competition. I am not going to tell you about what happens on Sunday: you wouldn't believe me. It is all the fault of the Sons of the Desert, Bonnie Scotland Tent.

As it happens I designed the logo for this strange bash. I have got a tie with the symbol what I drew on it. It is the ninth U.K. Convention of the Laurel and Hardy Fan Club. Calling it a fan club is too mild. The chaps, (and they are nearly all chaps) in this organisation take it all almost seriously which is why they call their organisation 'The Sons of the Desert' and why the various regional groups are known as 'Tents'. The Scottish one is known as the Bonnie Scotland Tent after the name of the movie in which the dynamic duo have acres of fun. There is a Grand Sheik in charge of it all and the members adorn themselves with fezzes. It is a super wheeze. Mr. Douglas Brown will be there, fez atop his gleaming cranium. I will practically guarantee that the schoolchildren whom Mr. Brown guides through their little scholastic careers do not ever suspect him of such weekend idiocy. Naturally Douglas does not let on about his leisure-time activities. It would not do for a schoolteacher to go about the corridors and his duty wearing a fez though to be honest there are a right few education officials for whom that would be appropriate dress and in fact Coco the Clown's outfit would be most suitable considering their antics from time to time.

It is not difficult to understand why Stan and Ollie can draw the response which sets up such a collection of bananas. It would be impossible with any other pair. Could you imagine a fan club for Abbot and Costello? Or Little and Large? Cannon And Ball? You could just as easily envisage a Bob Monkhouse fan club. God knows, there might actually be one of them, President care of Leverndale. Mind you, I once attempted to start up a Bill Sykes Fan Club. My pal Derek, the mad Italian psychiatrist from Kirkcaldy, said Bill was a much misunderstood chap. That was enough for me to be going on with.

But Laurel and Hardy stand out from all the others. For a start all the other comedy pairs have an idjit and a straight man. Jerry Lewis made funny faces and acted zany while Dean Martin looked on, handsome and debonair. I never liked Jerry Lewis. Even as a child I knew he was only ACTING daft just as you knew that the appalling Norman Wisdom wore expensive lounge suits and a businessman-like expression when he was off the screen and stage. But I loathed Dean Martin.

I always loathed the straight men. They were smug and complacent and pasty and had no talent of any kind whatsoever. They let the funny half of the act do all the work and make fools of themselves in public. I had no time for Ernie Wise for instance and it is a source of wonder to me that he has still got some kind of clout in the world of showbiz. If you think the short fat hairy one is a meretricious little mountebank just think of Mike Winters. Sweet Jesus, thinking of his brother Bernie is bad enough. Comedy duos are awful.

But Laurel and Hardy weren't like that. They were both daft and in their different ways. The great thing about Laurel was that he knew he was half – indeed quarter –

witted. The truly great thing about Hardy is that he thought he wasn't. The two of them got each other into the most splendid of fine messes all the time. What made you laugh was their innocence. I do not laugh at very much myself, (though I once actually wet myself during 'MONSIEUR HULOT'S HOLIDAY'), but Laurel and Hardy have never failed to get a response from a grin to a choke.

Off screen of course neither Stan Laurel or Oliver Hardy were like their stage personas. Laurel, for instance, was a heavy womaniser which sits oddly of a bloke who married the same woman three times. But then, all the stars lived somewhat lurid lives and if it wasn't women it was gambling or booze. Sometimes it was all three with dope as a side order. It is only idiots who imagine their heroes to be such in real life. There are a lot of idiots about however and the tabloids are filled with drivel which panders to public stupidity.

Talking of stupidity, there is a brand of it of which I am in favour. I am in favour of such chaps as fill their lives with enthusiasm for something essentially daft. I like stamp-collectors and model railway enthusiasts for instance. Film buffs and aeroplane obsessives. Blokes whose every waking hour keeps them at making lists of Top Ten chart successes. Bibliophiles. Butterfly collectors. All daft as brushes of course, but harmless. I mean REALLY harmless. I will bet you that none of the above have ever hit anybody with their heads. Their heads are reserved for other things.

In the case of the Sons of The Desert, Bonnie Scotland Tent, their heads this weekend will be mere vehicles for red fezzes, and for wine and song and movies and very silly games. I don't know about women. Generally women are too sensible for such capers, I am afraid, and they are more the losers for it too.

The Reek of Intolerance

LAST SATURDAY I encountered the rudest man I ever met. Stand up, Mr Stephen Campbell of this parish. Mr Campbell is one of the young Glasgow artists who have taken the art world by storm in recent years. In fact, Mr Campbell can be said to have spearheaded this so-called renaissance. Mr Campbell is reputed to earn as much as forty-five thousand quid for a painting. Though I find such a sum faintly absurd, generally my feeling about Mr Campbell obtaining lots of poppy is one of good luck to him. In short, until I met the fellow I bore no malice to him at all. Mr Campbell does not harbour a similar notion to myself as I was to find out last week. Before I had stuttered out a sentence he sanguinely informed me that I was scum, filth and ordure altogether. He told me to get away from him. He threatened violence either from himself or from another party. A second attempt on my part to converse and at least elicit the cause of his ire drew a second denouncement quite as florid as the first.

Now I have no idea what brought his tirade on unless it is that the art criticism which I do for a little Glasgow magazine, 'Culture City' has somehow upset him. He will doubtless disagree with much of what I have to say on art: lots of people do. It is certainly true that I am no admirer of his work and I have expressed that judgment from time to time. To be quite frank with you, not only do I think that I write better than he paints, I suspect that I *paint* better than he paints. I suppose such an impertinence on my part inclines Mr Campbell to a wariness upon first meeting me. Wariness is one thing. Outright boorishness is quite another.

But outright boorishness is somewhat of a growth industry, especially, I regret to say in that group of working-class origin among our educated classes and among what passes for our new intelligentsia. *Epater les bourgois* is all very well but should be confined to callow youth. After about the age of nineteen you should surely give it up.

No one expects the gentility of a Jane Austin drawing room from our young proletarian Glaswegerati and their artistic coevals. No one expects a show of such colourful contumely either. Were some of the prima donnas to embark on such behaviours in the average public house in, say, Drumchapel, they would soon, and effectively at that, be informed of the error of their ways. And the same working–class intelligentsia know it only full well.

But there is a quaint concept which some of our prole artistes seem to have that they should enjoy the lionisation of their well–bred hosts to the full by abusing their hospitality. I say quaint, because it is so. It is quaint and picturesque; just as is a peasants cottage complete with thatched roof. Never mind that the peasants themselves were damned glad to get out of such an encumbrance to their lives. Never mind that most decent working class people are more than ready to adopt bourgeois good manners if it means they get peace from a collection of the polloi who consistently try to bring us all to their own level.

I know, and many of you will have observed them for yourselves, a set of these people, these intellectuals of the old working class origin with their cliches culled from the inadequacy of their auto didactism. I could give you names of artists, playwrights, writers, even musicians, (although much more rarely, for musicians are generally a courtly people). I mind their behaviour, just as much as I minded the less than Corinthian spirit which I saw at the Scotland-Cyprus game this week, when some Scots fans boo–ed the Cyprus National Anthem. But I mind more than that.

I can't take to the underlying idea that all is fair in the class war and that people of different ideologies should be personally excoriated. There is no love lost politically between a certain Militant member whom I know and a certain Tory councillor with whom I am also friendly. But when the politics are over I have never met men more polite and genuinely decent towards each other. Opposition to tyranny is a noble thing: opposition to a courtesy between people of differing positions is a debasement. Now there's enough Voltairean pomposity to be going on with.

For there is more than the issue of manners here. One of the most reviled men in any British Parliament was Charles Stewart Parnell. He was never moved to a personal discourtesy. Passion is all very well but there has to be a scale of it and quite simply there has got to be a basic acceptance of the other's right to hold and express an opinion without descending to personal abuse. There may be some exceptions to this – Hitler comes to mind – but as a general principle it seems sound enough to me. Under Mr Campbell's bluster of the other week I can smell the overpowering reek of intolerance and a curiously dated cant. And there is not a trace of art in that.

Glittering Prizes

IF ANY PHRASE could possibly sum up the idiocy of the Turner Prize, that which purports to be the Art world's answer to the Booker Prize for Unreadable Books, it was the one I am about to reveal to you. And if the Booker Prize is for unreadable books, well the Turner Prize is for Unwatchable Art. The phrase in question came from that fat bloke, Humphrey Burton, the BBC man charged with the duty of presenting some programme about this kulchuring kontrast to the world of books. 'Sometimes,' incanted Burton breathlessly, 'this artist's work only lasts as long as water takes to dry'. We were then treated to a lengthy shot of the artist in question – a Mr Richard Long – pouring a pail of water down some bloody cliff in Patagonia just to make a pattern of the dampness on the rocks. I used to do that myself, but only when I was very wee. Then I didn't use a bucket though. And I didn't call it Art. The ordinary fellow doesn't get to call it Art these days either. Far from winning ten thou, he is likely to get fined fifteen notes if the Polis catch him committing the deed up a close.

But pouring water on the idea of real Art was not confined to this Long chap. Pouring water on it was the very concept behind the Turner Prize for Unwatchable Art, and indeed the Booker Prize for Unmentionable People, and most of the People I witnessed through the TV coverage of this Art payola scheme would be likely candidates for that.

The artists swanning about the Tate Gallery were in the main a pasty, mealy, pinched-face looking lot. You could tell them a mile off apart from those Art Administrators who now infest Kulcheral Developments. The administrators and so-called 'patrons' and other piranha are invariably pin-striped, wearing their hair genteely over-long, their faces bloated with rich food, their nostrils purple from sniffing fine wines; the self-satisfaction of the connoisseur standing out on their coupons like the flush of an alcoholic. The Director of the Tate was cavorting in front of the cameras trying to fit the description above, but there were others trying harder at that.

Plenty of celebs about too, there was. Bamber Gascoigne talked unreasonable rubbish and had clearly forgotten to squirt his hairspray around the locks. Malcolm McLaren – the fellow who gave us THE SEX PISTOLS don't y'know – was there too, representing the modish world of the street-wise guys. It was a heady mixture. Toffs, glue sniffers, and poetasters mingle easily, like Regency bucks and beggars in a Blue Ruin shop. A bint in blusher and a pair of glasses like a bent coathanger spoke highly of 'the Art.' More bints followed calling themselves Art Critics. Noticeably, none of the candidates were bints: In fact there was not a woman on the list.

The candidates were of course a joke. Yet another visual mountebank, this one named as a sculptor, showed his art off. The thing was made of linoleum and plywood; it closely resembled a poky hat unceremoniously stuck onto a child's toy, like the result of some ghastly misdemeanour in the nursery. Our presenter, Humphrey Burton said it was 'A metaphor for our senses.' The only sense I could think of was that of outrage. Humphrey Barton wondered aloud, he said, 'Is it an eye or is it perhaps a sperm.' I don't know about you but that last remark fell upon stony ground.

The next two revelations were two fellows who I remember were once told of as 'performance artists'. I recollect a young student at my Art College who went in for this nomenclature. He once stood for a day and a half on a box of earth, patiently explaining that he had planted seeds in the ordure beneath him and was letting, he said, 'the grass grow under his feet'. The examiners failed him of course: they, like any rational chaps, were looking for a decent stookie when it came to sculpture.

Gilbert and George were once performance artists but now they do a sort of easel picture show. The 'RADIO TIMES' said that they 'juxtapose military, royal and religious symbols with meths drinkers, immigrants, and skinheads. 'Woody Allen,' said the Radio Times, 'discussed their significance in MANHATTAN.' Well, what can I say; it takes the breath away. I thought their paintings looked as strange as they do – they both wear Dunn's Thornproof tweed suits with all three buttons done up – but the works looked as if somebody else, possibly Martians, had committed them.

Howard Godgkins' offering seemed to be the scraping of his palette knife off onto an old draining board. This was most perspicacious of me: that is what his painting was, and truth is a lot dafter that fiction.

The winner, Malcolm Morley, used to be what was called a Photo–Realist; that is, he squared up travel brochure photos and enlarged them onto canvas. As everybody who has ever studied art knows, this is an absolute dawdle. I know in particular: it was a wee trick of mine. Mr. Morley gets about £100,000 for these daubs. He does them upside down. Doing them upside down seems to increase the price 10,000 times. Not to worry. Lord Gowrie presented the cheque to Mr. Morley, who was actually in America not bothering about a measly ten grand. It is as well that Grey Gowrie is Minister for the garment industry. I never saw anybody before who could make a necktie look slept in.

But if Grey himself looked slept in, that was as nothing to the rumpled appearance of the Art, none of it more than the 'landscape' paintings of our intrepid water-pourer, Mr. Richard Long. In front of a large circle of, I swear this is true, mud from the River Avon, presenter Humphrey pronounced this insanity as 'beautiful'. Said Burton, a gasp of awe escaping from his over-ripe lips, 'the mud was put on with Long's very own hands!'. Surely boys, not by HIS OWN HAND! Can the human mind take so much ecstasy?

It is an odd thing. The truth is, lads that British Art has not blown its trumpet enough throughout the twentieth century, for it compares well enough with that of Europe, and the strident posturing of so-called American art, that naive expression of American imperialism circa the 1950's, must surely be darkened in its small corner by the brightness of the true art of our native land. Here is a wee list of prominent British artists still alive, if old, and each worthy of the sort of distinction one should give to those who have laboured long: Carel Weight, Patrick Proctor, Peter Blake, Michael Andrews, David Tindle, Edward Burra... the list goes on: and add to it some of the very fine artists who taught me in our own bit of the British Isles, Robin Philipson, David Michie, the wonderful Elizabeth Blackadder.

It was Ruskin who said of Whistler that he 'had thrown a pot of paint in the public's face'. None of the above-named

artists of my own little selection are likely to achieve the
public acclaim which this Turner Prize disgrace will
manage for the charlatans we saw the other night, more's
the pity. For the Turner prize can be summed up in that
glorious phrase of the telly man's. 'This artist's work,' it
went, 'only lasts as long as it takes water to dry'. But the
pot these artists turned over on us, the public,was not
water, and it was not paint; and it does not take a sense of
smell to tell its substance.

Politics and Politicians

Stranger than Fiction

THE FIRST INKLING I had that this was an age of fiction was, I can't remember, maybe the Lucan murder, or perhaps the disappearance of John Stonehouse. This was the first time I considered that reality was TV drama. That it was strange.

Nearly thirty years of my life had gone by and everything had been normal, like 'Mrs Dale's Diary' or 'Coronation Street' is normal. Then, as a child, films and books were fiction. Heroes had carved faces and clipped voices, villains had malignant evil written large across them, heroines were chaste, or at least, unobtainable. Fiction was not real life, and was intended to shape unreality.

The world was safe and fantasy, fiction, and danger of any kind was what you read before you went to sleep at night. That was when I was young.

The Lucan murder was like a detective story. It was tailor-made for Chief Superintendent Appleby to say: 'You remember the Lucan case, Brer Fox?' and for Fox to reply, 'Wasn't that when Lord Lucan did in the governess?', and to finish with: 'Never caught him, did we, Super? Vanished clean into thin air?'

The Lucan murder was pure English country house detective novel. Lucan himself didn't seem real. The outre 1950's clubs, the gaming rooms, the very look of him with his regular features and guards moustache, was all out of time. It was not real.

The Stonehouse disappearance was the same. It was like the blurb of the synopsis on the back of the old green Penguins – 'Famous MP disappears without a trace, seemingly committing suicide by walking into the sea. But when he surfaces months later in Florida he has a tale to tell – one which could embarrass top people, or topple the

Government!' None of it made sense, particularly when the emergent facts appeared to be far more mundane than seemed possible.

From them on reality started being fiction all the time. The Liberal Party was capable of providing more thrillers than a publisher's list. Peter Hain, in a celebrated case, was arrested for bank robbery. Hain was a fresh-faced young idealist, perfect for the role of bank-robbing doppelganger.

He was acquitted, and it looked as if the South African BOSS thugs had tried to set him up. BOSS were later to figure in the trial, for attempted murder, of the leader of the Liberal Party. The leader himself looked like an exaggeration on the part of the casting department; like Eric Porter in a British 'B' movie.

Not much came of it except that lots of Liberals seemed to be lying their heads off, and the Liberal Party got a new leader of the most respectable ordinariness who was later to preside over an alliance with a new and unlikely political party formed by a failed politician now calling himself a statesman. Evelyn Waugh could have written that.

There were lots of failed politicians in the Age of Fiction though, and a few of them gave themselves the 'statesman' tag. It is a measure of the intellectual rigour of this Government that Edward Heath should be less and less remembered for the botch-up he made of running the country.

There was, if you recollect, the TV curfew, the three-day-week; you drank in pubs at night by candlelight because there was no electricity. It was cold then when I went home to my bedsit at night, and I sat with my feet inside the gas oven to keep warm.

Five trade unionists were sent to jail, but the Government invented another very old law, and somebody to pay the fine, and the trade unionists were released. There were tanks at Heathrow. This was a script by early

Graham Greene. It was not real.

Every style of fantasy was being enacted out in the streets of real life. More moles were unearthed in Whitehall than Smiley could ever have uncovered. Sir Anthony Blunt was revealed as a traitor, despite his appointment to the Queen. Nobody had thought fit to tell us.

While poor old Vassal had been doing his stretch, the good Sir Anthony had been living splendidly in his town house and being quite the aesthete. But then, every new mole who emerged seemed to be a fat cat as well.

The newest adventure story for little boys brings us into the world of Erskine Childers, set in the South-Atlantic. This time around the story centres on Britain being at war with a hostile foreign power – a semi banana republic run by a fascist military junta, all thin moustaches and gold epaulettes.

There are no jobs for two out of three school-leavers, and over 3,000,000 on the dole. The war will cost countless millions of pounds and soldiers and sailors on both sides will lose their lives. Given a half-decent Labour Opposition the Government would have fallen, but the Prime Minister, a grocer's daughter with predictably strong suburban middle-class views, makes sure that her government can survive by pressing the jingoism button.

Unemployment doesn't seem to matter so much now. We are at war, backs to the wall. It doesn't even matter either that we won't get Jenkin's ear back: the war is not for that. The Government will be returned with an increased majority at the next election. This is an age of fiction, the cheaper the better.

It is blood and thunder, and Mills and Boon romance. It is, they say, for real though. I do not believe anything I am told anymore. It is all fiction. There is altogether, as Big Daddy said, a powerful smell of mendacity about. Nothing is real, and anyway I don't believe it.

Lament for a Lost Cause

I SAW the television pictures of the men going back this week and if you are looking for a fun-packed column today you have, to paraphrase Presley, come to the wrong place. Oh, I had intended to treat you to a spirited discourse on the state of the Battlefield Rest. But I do not feel spirited now, not even over The Rest.

I know that some of you felt that I was not entitled to my recent espousal of the miners' cause, or that the Herald was not entitled to allow it. Or even that you were not entitled to get my opinions thrust down *your* throat. I hope I do not do that and I hope you will continue reading this, even if you disagree with me. I want you to finish this column to the bitter end, not because I am any better – for I am not – in arguing any argument at all over this tragic dispute than Arthur Scargill, or Mick McGahey, or, if it comes to that, than Jimmy Reid. But for a raddled old cynic like your Urban V, it is strange how much I want to say what I feel. That is a strange thing; that has the queer smell.

I damn near cried when I saw the television pictures: There was a lump in my throat the size of a pit-head bath. When the men went back to work the worst thing was the bands. Grimethorpe had their world-famous brass band marching their men into work.

They were small men with pinched faces, faces grim and beaten and proud. At his own pit Arthur Scargill, his bouffant strangely defeated, looked lined and drawn enough to die. I can see the words in the history books now. 'After the collapse,' the words will read, 'Scargill died two years later, a broken man.'

By God they have done that often enough to the leaders of working people; those with brains and flair and guts enough to necessitate the full panoply of what, for want of a better insult, you could call the State.

I think my newspaper did better than most during the strike; few behaved as fairly. That great journalist, and a good man too, James Cameron, died during the dispute, before he could witness the ignominy and humiliation shown in the television films of this rerun of 1926.

Cameron wrote it himself in his own vacillating blatt The Guardian: 'The miners,' wrote Jimmy, 'are of course utterly right, and they must win if the British sense of civilisation is to survive.' James Cameron himself did not survive. He would have felt the shame and indignation too.

I saw the television pictures: I saw the brave bands at the heads of the columns. There was a disgraceful professor who advanced the theory not a few months ago that the 'reason' for the 'violence' of the picketing miners was that 50 years ago the cleverer and brainier miners ensured that their sons did not follow them down the pits and instead became clerks, salesmen, teachers, and lecturers like himself.

Thus remained, said the learned professor, the dross; literally the untermensch to work down the mines with their unimaginative ways, only capable of the toil of beasts of burden underneath the earth. It is just as well though I suppose that we have the untermensch: you cannot eat a lecture. Anyway I saw the television pictures. The miners did not look like Harijans: they looked like men to me.

There were those in this Government who saw the miners as untouchables though: certainly as natural enemies. The year-long strike cost so many billions we could have kept the pits open for the next 20 years without a closure at all.

Ach, it is not difficult to fathom where the victory was at all. Did not Nigel Lawson speak of taking on the miners as 'a good investment?' They Tory Molochs have been planning this for years. First the miners: now for the rest of us.

But sure, was it not in the miners' best interests that we closed their jobs down anyway: rotten, nasty, brutish way of life altogether. Would be a lot better off in the healthy fresh air outside the Jobcentres. There seem, oddly enough, few

116

objections to those chaps from Nottinghamshire getting a wee dose of the old pneumoconiosis. There is a positive reek, my dears, of old-fashioned humbug about the place.

I saw some other pictures on television this week. In a programme about the development of TV news coverage I saw films of those dark days in Selma, Alabama back in the '50s when I was a boy.

I saw the police and militia club down women and children for their silent black protest. I saw Martin Luther King tell the people that he had a dream, saw Kennedy shot down, saw, and remembered, the veiled face of Jacqueline Kennedy at that funeral. There was a lump in my throat then too.

The last time I remember tears welling up behind my eyes in front of a TV set was when Elvis Presley died and I remembered something of, I suppose, my heritage. This week too, when I saw the pictures of the men going back I remembered a lot more of my heritage than merely Elvis, and I could have wept for myself as much as for those humbled but proud men who have just gone back with the bitter taste of defeat in their throats.

Remember the War?

THE WAR lasted six years: it lasted even longer for me. It lasted longer for everybody. From the time I was bloody born it was nothing but the war. Standing in the middle of the streets clutching my mum's skirts and bored into oblivion by the thirty-five minute conversation these grown-ups were having outside Cochrane's the grocers, the words were repeated like a mantra. Before the war. After the war. During the war. The war, the war. Everything was about the war.

Shopping was about the war. There were still the same shortages. You couldn't get sardines, for instance. One day, a huge advert appeared on a nearby hoarding. 'Skippers are

117

back!' it announced in triumph. A couple of weeks later we had sardines on toast for the first time. I couldn't see what the fuss was about. Later we got baked beans with a piece of gristle, said to be pork, in the middle of the tin.

My dad was Olympian on the matter of such foods and insisted on potatoes or a rasher or a slice of liver. He was buggered, he said, if he'd come back to anything other than a proper dinner, not like that Mr. Black next door who had, claimed my father, a banana for his tea.

Incidentally, the banana was of recent date because the first time I saw a banana was in the school when a wee girl had brought in two for the rest of the kids to see. Her uncle had brought them back from his last voyage. The bananas were displayed in every classroom and then the top class got a slice of the unpeeled fruit to sample. The humble banana was more exotic than a Kiwi fruit is today. Three years later poor Mr. Black next door was being held in contempt for his nightly consumption of one.

Everything was rationed of course. The then Labour government liked rationing in much the same way that the Roundheads enjoyed plain linen rather than lace and drab serge rather than velvet suits. When Dior brought in the new look in 1947, Harold Wilson, then at the Board of Trade, took a hairy because of the extra cost of the material. Women voted out the Labour Party in 1951 because the Socialists had no logical attitude to lingerie and the like. They stopped the rationing of sweets in 1953. Sweets were then boiled sweets. Bullseyes and black-striped balls and soor plooms and sherbet dabs. It could have been 1938. It was.

I went to school wearing a pair of short trousers cut down from an old pair of suit strides of my dads. I had grey Banner shirts which had been on my uncle's back in the early thirties. Everybody looked like something out of a William book. The girls wore gymslips and had pig-tails up till the age of sixteen. You got hit quite a lot and never spoke back in adult company and were, oddly enough, much happier than the weans of today seem to be. For a start you generally got left alone to be weans.

That's another thing adults were much nicer then. I remember myself and my wee brother and my mother all going down, late at night, on the train to Stevenson to see my Grandma who lived there. The compartment (there were still compartments then with seaside scenes on the walls and straps on the windows) was filled with a collection of squaddies (there were lots of squaddies about then too). They gave my mother a seat and put us on their knees and taught me how to play Snap as raucously as possible, undermining at every play any sort of quiet discipline my mother tried to impose. A big fellow let me sit on the netting above the seats and I fell asleep and was woken up at Saltcoats.

But then adults were much nicer to adults then. My uncle Tom, who was a raging capitalist, voted Labour because he thought that everybody should get a better deal. Mrs. Thatcher's Victorian morality may have replaced Harold MacMillan's spirit of Dunkirk but it has not replaced it for the better. It was not, in retrospect, all like that. There were still, as had happened in the First World War, a lot of hard-faced men who had done well out of this one and my father was one of the luckless men who did badly out of it. He'd been a regular soldier before the war and had came back to discover all sorts of fly boys taking his job. Something those born 10 years after me will not know: we were poor then.

It was maybe 1956 when things changed. I was only a kid and it was utterly bemusing. Motor cars were black boxy things with running boards and only toffs had them. Policemen tackled crime on bicycles. Homes had old furniture or, at the most modern, utility stuff which was, erroneously as things turned out, much despised. The wireless was a nightly entertainment and every house had a green baize card table. Supper consisted of Ovaltine or Bourneville cocoa and thinly spread Marmite on toast. The men worked till very late at night and on Saturday mornings. The pictures were big and so were the weekly encounters at the library. It was, in my memory, just like the Hovis adverts. What's wrong with that?

Nothing at all really. Except that what happened was that we were still living in the pre-war days when the rest of Europe was recognising that there really was a new world to build out there. While Europe was re-building its industry we were still messing about being as class-ridden, and as quickly as possible too, as we had been before the war forced a sort of democracy on us all. And I'm part of that. The war baby. None of us ever really grew up.

TV and Radio

That Hogmanay Show

PAT CHALMERS was late. The self-styled senior executives of BBC Scotland sat waiting in their olive leatherette executive-style chairs for the Controller of Scotland. Chalmers was a stickler for punctuality: he liked to play the boss. (He was reputed to dress, at least in his mind, in uniform; epaulettes, golden lanyards, glittering orders at the breast, an Iron Cross second class nestling at the throat.)

Chalmers being late was an unhealthy augury for what the Controller of Beeb Scotus had himself described as a 'crisis meeting.' 'The sod is making us sweat,' thought each high-powered self-styled BBC senior executive as he sweated. Each in turn thought of lighting up a fag or pouring a glass of water from the carafe in front of him, but thought better of it. 'Makes you look nervous,' each thought, a collective epiglottis welded to the tonsils with fear-wracked aridity, a collective gasp for a gasper.

Suddenly in strode the fearless Duce of Queen Margaret Drive, striding, it is true, a trifle gingerly with his arse red raw from the thrashing he had just received from the Fuehrer, the Director-General himself. 'To work!' cried Benito Chalmers, 'Gentlemen, to work!', as he cautiously lowered his rear into his throne at the head of the table. 'I want to know the man responsible for this fiasco!' he screamed.

'I'll have the bastard tarred and feathered for this,' he shrieked. 'I'll have him run out on a rail! Knee-capped. Made to drink in the BBC Club with Clifford Hanley.' The scarlet-faced Duce uttered one final threat and imprecation. 'I'll have him transferred to Highland!' At that he slumped back. 'I want the thing responsible for that outrage, that, that...' words failed The Glorious Leader, 'That Hogmanay...' He ended lamely and forlornly.

121

The self-styled senior BBC executives looked about wildly, and cudgelled their brains: how could they possibly explain to their now apoplectic boss that the very chap responsible for the most risible Hogmanay show of all risible Hogmanay shows was none other than the purple-faced Prince of Spleen, Mr Pat Chalmers himself? They began to slide, rather hysterically, out of any possible charge of complicity.

One said he was on a junket, I mean covering the crucial elections in San Marino at the time; another said he had been away distorting the coverage of the pickets at a nearby colliery; others claimed domestic upheavals on the crucial dates; a high-up chap brandished a note from his mum written on a piece of a butcher paper bag.

'YOU FOOLS,' screamed Lord Chalmers. 'You blithering, blathering scum. Why do they send me a pack of dolts like this?' wept Mr Bokassa-Chalmers, tearing the suave grey hairs out of his temples. 'Do you think I care who MADE that bloody programme? I knew it was rubbish from beginning to end. What in God's name d'you expect when you shove such a collection as Tom O'Connor, John Grieve, or Moira Anderson. Moira Anderson?... I mean, MOIRA ANDERSON...'

At this, Chalmers began to laugh uncontrollably. 'Moira, ha ha, Moira ha ha ha... Ander... Ha ha ha he ho ho ho... with the old wrap-around full-length tartan skirt ha ha ha... that upwardly-mobile accent right out of Spam Valley ha ha... wee Mrs Electricity Board and her Fitted Kitchen... 'John Anderson My Jo' sung in Bearsdenese, 'ha ha ha he he ho ho ha...' gasping for breath, the Queen Margaret Drive Supremo coughed until he was sick.

Wiping the tears from his eyes, Chalmers swiftly narrowed them. 'Who,' he demanded in his famous Let's-get-to-the-nub-of-the-problem voice, 'thought of that Tom O'Connor?' Instant denials sped across the Wipe-Kleen simulated french-polish boardroom table.

122

There was a faint, fearful cough from a nearby minion. 'We had Rolf Harris one year,' said the underling almost under his breath, 'Strewth, don't I know it!' exploded the Golden Boy of Broadcasting. 'I saw it myself. Though I was having the DTs. It couldn't have been worse if you'd had pink bloody kangaroos hopping across the screen. Seeing the New Year in with a bloody wobble board. A little bit here and a little bit there...' mimicked Chalmers cruelly.

'But,' continued the beloved sage of Broadcasting House, 'the Hogmanay Show is always awful and what do you expect? Even if you did get chaps like Chic Murray or indeed Andy Cameron, Hector Nicol, Alex Norton and the boys from the old 7:84, wee Phil McCall; even if you got them they'd never get given their head.'

'We could even have shoved on some daft and nostalgic wee clips of Robert Wilson or Sid McEwan or that old josser with the curly stick; we could have had outside visits to boozers earlier on that day to see the celebrations and a film of the celebrants on the top deck of a Drumchapel bus, and interviews with eminent foreigners and a lot more poppy spent and scenes of the bevvy artists round the Mercat crosses, and that Urban Voltaire shouting incoherently at his TV set...' The Controller of BBC Scotland (and next - The World), paused for breath. 'But what I want to know is,' he said, 'is WHO IS RESPONSIBLE FOR NETWORKING THIS YEAR'S DRIVEL?'

The door suddenly opened and in walked a slim elegant chap who is not as baldy as all that really. 'You were responsible, pal,' said the Urban Voltaire, for it was he, 'and guys like you every year, for our annual humiliation in front of the English.' And at that sally, your man casually bounced the luckless boss out of the boardroom before coolly taking the chair.

'Gentlemen,' he said, striking a match off the head of a nearby senior BBC executive, 'is there any drink going in this place at all before we get started?'

Desert Island Discs

IT IS ONE of the major regrets of my life so far that I never got on DESERT ISLAND DISCS. I'll bet it's one of yours too. Like you, I have been listing and re-listing my records for years, and internally answering, in the suavest possible ways, old Roy's urbane questions. Well, the old bugger's gone now, more's the pity, and where could they find a replacement for him among todays crass broadcasters? Radio Scotland had a tentative idea along similar lines not so long ago and even approached me as a possible guest to kick it off. I had the MOST surprising records, I can assure you, and lots of boasts to go along with them for the talking bits. Like many things to do with your Urban V, the Lord of Despair and Self-Pity, it came to naught, but now that Roy has kicked the bucket Beeb Scotus might just reconsider. I am ready and waiting for the call. I will even don the white tuxedo to give the first programme an ineffable air of sophistication if not respectability.

I was intrigued all the same to learn of the circumstances by which Mr. Plomley had thought up this marvellous programme. It transpires that Roy had been working his wee bum off for some years trying to think of some super wheeze for a programme every week, and wanted to find something which might just last for perhaps six programmes to give him a little respite. Six programmes which could give him a chance to get a wee drink in, and space to live. His idea didn't last six weeks. It lasted forty-three years. I still never got on it, mind.

Plomley's skill as the one and only presenter was not totally due to his astonishing politeness. (Anybody who ever heard Roy's programme with Otto Preminger, the American film director has to admire such a politenesss: it was beyond the call of normal duty). Plomley's politeness was so catching that I once heard Johnny Rotten of the notorious SEX PISTOLS reduced to describing his schooldays with affection. Plomley had more than courtesy.

Roy Plomley was the sort of polite Englishman who has probably disappeared since the war. He brought manners to a level of education and imagination which successive politicians have been trying to outlaw for years. If I, like you, have been irritated by all the marble-mouthed knickers-in-a-twist Oxbridge idjits what have gone on the wireless and the telly for over forty years, (since the war – it was worse before as well), Roy Plomley never annoyed you. You took his accent and old-fashioned courtesy for granted, like Alastair Cook and good old-established firms. You knew that the very notion which became ISLAND was inspired, and thanked God on your bended knees that such a glorious programme had such a magnificent host. Think of how it could have been: of how it could be now. Think of the alternatives to Roy; do.

If there is one especially awful thing about that poisonous wee box in the corner of the living room, there is a lot more. They are called TV 'Personalities'. I, like everybody else with an I.Q. of over thirty, hate them. I despise them. (I envy them as well, but never mind that). Think of objects. Michael Parkinson is as Yorkshire as an old slice of black pudding – a very old piece of black pudding. Parkinson is a Yesterday's Man if ever I saw one. Noel thing, can't remember his name, Edmonds, that's it, is a dod of processed white bread, a slim Baco-foiled triangle of Dairylea Cheese Spread. The list of dreadful tellyfaces into the interviewing goes on. And a perfectly horrid list it is too. There is even worse than the foregoing.

There is a class of Tellyperson who, like Roy Plomley, had ideas for programmes. Most of the programmes are sort of games or, anyway, sort of something. The mistress of all this was that Esther Rancid, (whose hubby, I note, a Mr Desmond Wilcox, was deputising as a columnist for a Scottish Sunday rag the other week. He was deputising for yet another English erk, Mr. Bernard Falk. Rags go in for

English Erks straight off the cathode ray tube. Rags and telly are in cahoots in their cultural lobotomising operations). Since Esther whatever-her-name-is had the bright notion of patronising the lumpen proles out there, thousands of other Tellypersons have followed in her wake.

There are now programmes called, I believe, 'THE PRICE IS RIGHT' and 'GAME FOR A LAUGH', and all of them have hosts called Jeremy Beadle or Geoffrey Kelly or anyway something like that. I can't be expected to know their bloody names. All of them, male or female, have the same faces: they each have high profile teeth and an endless supply of the good-humour of lunacy. They all seem to have persuaded TV companies of the efficacy of their ideas for programmes. Roy Plomley would have had as much chance with Lord Grade as Galileo had with the Pope.

I too once had a wee notion for a telly programme. I based it on Mr. Plomley's show. It was a sort of DESERT ISLAND DISCS but with bits of movies instead of records. The favourite bits of your favourite films: that was the idea. It is of course impossible. For a start, the film companies would doubtless charge a whole year's budget for one clip from 'GONE WITH THE WIND'. The other problem is that everybody would choose the same clips, starting with GONE WITH THE WIND and Rhett Butler saying : 'Frankly, Scarlet, I don't GIVE a damn'. Gene Kelly would be drenched to the skin once more and singing in the rain, Sam would be playing it again in Rick's Bar, Cagney would be top of the world Ma, Bette Davis would be taking a lit fag off Paul Henreid and saying bugger the world when we have the stars. It was a rotten idea really. I took it off Roy Plomley.

To get back to Roy Plomley. 'DESERT ISLAND DISCS' was a great idea which couldn't go wrong, and it had a man behind it to ensure that it didn't. There was another aspect to it's charm: it lasted so long. The programme had been on for more than my lifetime: you just expected it to go on forever. Modern day thinking – especially in the media – doesn't like the notion of anything going on forever. It upsets notions of New Technology. Plomley didn't like the tradition of the new, though he was too polite to say so. I wish he was still here, and his programme. At least until I got a chance to go on it myself.

Christmas and New Year

The Teachers' New Year

THAT WAS the teachers' New Year: yesterday it was. As it happens I invented the very phrase, though not the reality. It is some years back that I came up with the title and it has stuck. For a week or more the publicans of the city have looked towards but not forward to the bacchanalia the dominies enact on the final, lousing day: them with the next six weeks off too. It has long been a grievance with members of the public – who have increased the length of THEIR holidays while the teachers have had theirs shortened over the years – I say it has been a case for envy and resentment that the teachers get the long summer holidays that they do. The teachers are well due it and I will tell you that the last fortnight is spent with the black cloud of depression upon them and the feeling that they are going back to prison at the end of it.

I remember weans saying that school was a prison, but at least they went back home at night. It's the teachers who are prisoners: I did a 20 year stretch myself. The first 10 years I didn't know it. I had a grand time and I thought, poor fool as I was, that I wasn't only free: I thought I was practically the governor. The last 10 years was hard labour and the last two were in solitary. Jimmy Boyle doesn't know he was born. He covered himself with his own excrement. I spent the last five years copiously smeared in shit from weans and advisers and inspectors and bosses and the public at large. But I have divested myself from the raiment of educational ordure. I retired. Left. Got to ****. I got over the barbed wire fence. These days I keep coming across other retired teachers. We fall upon each other's necks like PoWs who have managed to get to Sweden or Switzerland. Freedom at last and yet I couldn't resist a final fling and the last at that. I went out on the teachers' New Year.

128

It is a disgrace the teachers' New Year is. Oh I don't mean the drunkenness and the ability to get beyond four o'clock without falling down and getting back home and falling asleep with your head on the plate and waking up in the morning imagining you have been beaten up by Millwall supporters, a notion substantiated by the blood all over your pillow, before you realise that the plate you had your head in also contained a litre of tomato ketchup.

Oh I don't mean that at all. I mean the maudlin recklessness which allowed the pedagogues to buy a round of drinks and then be sick in the toilet of Babbity Bowsters or the raucous singing or the unpleasantness with the taxi driver. I mean the fact that teaching has become so bloody awful that the dominies celebrate their summer freedom like lifers on parole. As it happens the teachers by and large say it ain't as awful as all that: they say I exaggerate. They whistle loudly in the dark. Tunelessly and with an air of resignation.

They have got a lot to resign themselves to. The years ahead for a start. I reckon it is going to take 10 years before some vestige of sanity comes back into the teaching profession. Ten years when the weans will run even more amok than they do at present and the public get fed up with anarchy on the streets. This has been a bad year for the teachers.

Sure, a lot of them get more money following the settlement last year. A fair amount of principal teachers voted to accept last year's deal on the basis that they would be rich and sod anybody else (the collective term for a group of principals is 'a lack' of them). Well God rot them. They got took. The public don't know this but the teachers now have to do extra hours called 'planned activity time.' The Government and the local authorities invented this as a punishment for going on strike in the first place. I never heard of any other union which organised more work and went to it with a will, but anyway that is nothing to me: I'm out.

In the meantime a collection of elected representatives tried to make life impossible for the dominies by closing and then not closing schools and the teachers started telling lies about how wonderful the school they were in was. It was ludicrous: one minute the teachers were telling you that the schools were hell itself and the next they were implying that their shop was practically bloody Eton College. The teachers made me sick. Strathclyde region tried to close every school that had a uniform, Latin, and nice well-behaved children on the basis that the lumpen proletariat were the salt of the earth and the entire populous should be like all them and go to academies the main function of which was to get up the stick as soon as possible if you were a girl and shoot heroin if you weren't. This is called socialism with a very stupid face.

A wee boy called Mick Forsyth started up an idea by which all sorts of thick parents would get to run the schools and manage to unite right and left because the lefty liberal parents don't like teachers and imagine they're as well educated anyway. Parents make me sicker than teachers do. Lefty liberals can induce terminal vomiting if I had to think about it.

This was the year that every career-minded lame brain jumped at the chance of getting up the ladder by starting up a load of mince called Standard Grade. I am not going to tell you anything about it except to say that if you are a parent you should be getting ready to take your weans out of the education system and putting them up the Dickensian chimneys where they will probably learn more.

This is the year that everybody who gets early retirement got it including the director of education himself. Eddie Millar has decided to spend the rest of a hopefully long life doing good works to make up for what he did directing education in the past few years. This year I saw sense and got out and this is the very last end-of-term report I will ever make. I've got a slight hangover from the teachers' New Year of yesterday. It is as nothing to the hangover from the past two decades drunk as I was with education.

Britain is Closed

'I NOTE, Mrs. Heraghty,' I said, as ever rather pompously, in my little South-Side club, 'that the powers that be have decided to close all district council museums and art galleries on Boxing Day and on January 2nd.' Turning to address the lieges I informed them that there would be no visits to Kelvingrove or the Burrell. The delights of the People's Palace and the Transport Museum would be shut off from them. The notion of taking their appalling offspring away to Haggs Castle children's museum was not an option and they will just have to put up with the squalling brats on their own and without a wee diversion for the merry little minds. 'What is more,' I told the gaping topers, 'a curator warned that the council will start closing the museums for every public holiday and was by no means happy with the prospect'. As it happens I am not surprised at this new move in killing joy.

I am not surprised at all. We British are made of sterner stuff than those foreign knaves who go in for all that raucous holiday mood when a wee break from work comes up. We celebrate our festivals in a splendidly British way: we close ourselves down. We close every shop, we close the pubs and restaurants if we can. Sometimes we chain up park gates. A public holiday is in fact a celebration of the nuclear family. Sometimes I think I'd rather have a nuclear war than a nuclear family. The public holiday is for a day with the weans and the boulder rolled in front of the cave. I know you are going to tell me that you can get your entertainment in the house in front of the cave. I know you are going to tell me that you can get your entertainment in the house in front of the television set. Television is for people who don't know how to make real life interesting and need the stimulus of flickering images made by other fraudulent mountebanks to jag up their dreary lives a little. A public holiday is designed to reinforce such a notion and depress the few rare intelligences such as your Urban V here.

Christmas and New Year are especially vile examples of holidays of course. I have said it every year in this column and I would suggest that just about everybody agrees with me - the festive season is about as rollicking as a jeremiad from Norman Tebbit. The week before Christmas is marked by the following: a thin miasma of drizzle at all times, a three-quarter hour wait for a taxi because the idjits are using them all, pub closing at nine o'clock – to let the bar staff go home of course – and the pubs anyway infested by amateurs who know not how to hold their liquor and who ludicrously imagine that they are Brendan Behan on a spree in New York. You cannot get a table in the restaurant and anyway all they are doing is Turkey followed by that teeth-welding confection, the Christmas pudding. To add the final insult you will be forced to parade through this incubus buying spurious baubles for people you only see twice a year. Gloomily you realise that they are doing exactly the same, An especially atrabilious note can be struck by the sight of tired women in shabby coats struggling through the town with vast parcels of toys that they cannot afford because, as is the way with the British proletariat, 'ye cannae let the weans dae without'.

Now I will guarantee you here that there are going to be readers who swipe at my misanthropy and who are right now forming the word 'killjoy' on their pursed lips. But it is not I who is the killjoy: far from it. I am your actual bon vivant, a chap for his grub and a potion to go with it. I like to see people cheery and outgoing. In short, I like to see the grown-ups in the pub, just as long as I am in it too. Now I do not know if you have noticed it yourselves but there is an increasing po-faced puritanism going the rounds regarding that great British institution, the public house.

Just as Thatcherite notions of freedom are being propounded it is astonishing how much freedom the same notions are taking away. Oh, I am not just talking about the official secrets act. I am talking about the collective freedoms; the very freedom to collectivise at all. Mrs. T does not like collectives unless it is a board of directors. She doses not like trade unions. Her followers do not like pubs or the idea of them. People in pubs talk you see. Heaven knows what dangerous philosophies can be promulgated in pubs. We should be sitting at home opening cans of fizzy beer instead and not bothering our little heads about the nation.

Dark tales there are about the evils of strong drink. Councillors and MP's who live in Edinburgh's New Town are talking gaily of refusing late licenses because 'it has got out of hand'. Depute Town Clerks refuse all day Sunday drinking and impose cheerless Sunday afternoons though anybody with a will can go and get rat-arsed in a club. Only those with a particular commitment to alcohol can get a drink in fact. One wonders, one does, how do they manage it on the continent? How do the French in their cities manage to cope with cafes open till three and four in the morning? And the Germans, the Italians, the Spanish, the... the list is endless. How do they manage to have shops open on public holidays ? Why do they insist on celebrating by celebrating?

I put these musings to Mrs. Heraghty. 'Disgraceful state of affairs, Anna. By the way,' I said, 'what's happening on Boxing Day?'. Anna did not look me in the eyes. 'I was thinking of clo...' I choked on the small goldie. 'Arghhhh' I cried and went out with murder in my heart.

OK, So I am a Killjoy

LAST YEAR it was that the weans wanted transformers. It's always something. One year it was cabbage patch dolls. I do

133

not – I still don't that is – know what a cabbage patch doll is. I know that they were greatly prized by small girls and that perhaps a squillion parents were wetting themselves in case they couldn't get a cabbage patch dolly for their little princess because their little treasure would kick up fifty levels of **** if such a plaything were not in her insensate little mitts by six-thirty on a Christmas morn. Last year though it was transformers.

Last year I went to a toy shop and insisted on seeing this transformer thing. I wanted to know what in heaven's name it was. Somehow I imagined it to be one of those electric sort of junction boxes that came with the Hornby Dublo train sets which you gazed at in wonderment in the Clyde Model Dockyard when you were a kid yourself. The lady in the toy shop brought out this plastic gee-gaw. I was patient with the lassie. 'Naw,' I said, 'a transformer,' I said, 'for the nephew,' I said. I mean, it wasn't for me was it? The lassie in the shop had been used to many an avuncular looking chap coming in with the same request and ignorance. 'This IS a transformer,' she said with hardly a trace of boredom. Then she explained what it transformed. It transformed itself from a sort of plastic model of a sort of car into a sort of small plastic dinosaur. It obviously also transformed perfectly sensible adults with nephews into idjits from whom money is easily parted. I quickly transformed myself into an out and out killjoy and buggered off to J. Smith and Sons where I bought every little beast books instead. That'll learn them. It will too.

Oh, I am ever the puritanical killjoy this time of year. You will not get me whistling jolly carols or putting up the Christmas decor. I am not your man for the Yuletide cheer and I shall not be wassailing any more than I do at any other time and in fact maybe less because the bloody boozers take it into their heads to close early or even all day so that families of this world can roll the boulders of their huddled wee caves into place and say goodbye to Humanity in the name of peace and goodwill to all men. There is a very good reason why the two or three days of Christmas are days of (generally) World Peace: nobody sees each other.

I am definitely a killjoy over such a farrago and such a celebration of consumerism. The fond mamas and papas are by far the worst. There are families going into hock right now because 'well – ye cannae disappoint the weans at Christmas.' You can and you should. Self-improving books and a sound beating to go with it: that is the very stuff to get this country back on an even keel. If you buy the books I am prepared to lead a national task force for the doings.

There is also a notion abroad that Christmas is the weans day. Ask any parent in with the kids all twenty-four hours. Every day is the weans day, they will tell you. Since when did the children start to count more than grown-ups? I suspect it began not that long ago when people stopped growing up at all. But there you are, did I not say I was a killjoy and a shockin' misanthrope altogether?

Now I will tell you this: there is many a chap and chapette who will say that I am twitting to you lot out there about my less than festive attitude. They will say that it is a con on my part. These are the fellows who simply refuse to believe that ANYBODY can be sensible about brats and bratettes. They will even point out that I do not actually eat weans or spread – as Baudelaire once claimed he did – the brains of new-born babies on breakfast toast rather like gentleman's Relish. Such people will even deride me with a dreadful calumny: they say that weans like ME.

Of course weans like me. I don't mess them about all year and then spend hundreds of spondulicks on them one day of the year. My attitude is that I will generally leave them in peace if they will do the same to me. If you will allow a certain pomposity from your Urban V here: lots of parents and other adults out there neglect their weans, and lots of

135

them indulge them and most of you seem to do a bit of both. A healthy neglect on the part of both parents and brats would do more good. I am going to get all this printed as a tract and go round doors asking for money for a spiritual rebirth. The Rev. Stewart Lamont can help me. He only gets a third of the profits though. I thought of the scam first.

But back to the beginning. I am not a pretend Christmas misanthrope. I am for real. I'm dreaming of a Black Christmas. (Crivven's. I have probably offended the Race Relations industry with that). Thus it is that you shall be hearing my soft persuasive voice over the air this Christmas morning if you tune into Radio Scotland. They are doing a kind of up-dated Christmas Carol. I was typecast, my dears. I am to be Scrooge. I shall delight in it.

However, if you think I make a perfect Scrooge, look to Strathclyde Regional Council. Their salaried workers are to be paid on their last day which will be after the weekend with but a day to go for the purchase of Christmas gifts. In a perverse way I applaud their decision. That is the first praise I ever gave to a gauleiter. Well it is the time of goodwill to all men.

Places

Land of My Fathers

THIS WAS A FINE WAY to get to the land of my ancestors: dead. By the alacrity of the motor car which Jimmy the photographer was driving it was the likeliest way of getting there. It is one thing doing the World Speed Record on salt flats but it is quite another doing it on the Oban road. By the time we got to the Mull Ferry I was prepared for death by a thousand cuts and would have looked forward to drowning as at least a gentle process. On the Mull ferry I discovered at least one chap who was prepared to drown himself with ferocity. I was meeting my first Mull Islander. Colin his name was and he was just back from holiday in Spain. Funny how you never think of a Highland man going to holiday in Spain. It's like imagining a flamenco dancer going to Stevenston.

Colin was a large, raw-boned, very drunk, bloke with a soft island accent, big blond moustaches, shoulder length hair and a capacity for a dram in him. Dram or not he spoke at length about the island we were just about to put our keelie feet upon. He told us that Mull was populated almost entirely by pop stars who planted trees everywhere: said Phil Collins of Live Aid fame had a huge house down the south of the island near Bunessan. He also told us that the biggest employers on Mull – the Sawmill – had been burned down recently. Colin worked in the sawmill and didn't seem to mind in the slightest. There was also a Yank on the boat.

As anybody who travels anywhere in our native land will discover there is always a Yank. This one was a pleasant old josser, looking for his Highland roots, determined to find out where his great granpappy Hector came from. He was a McLean too. Who was I to deride him? I was doing the same. This was the island from which my grandfather and my grandmother came. Neither of whom I ever saw, for they had been long dead before I was born. I have never even seen a faded sepia photograph of my dead grandfather, him who had died on the beaches of Gallipoli, a name in the remembrance book in Glasgow Cathedral. Highland Heritage my arse. Gallipoli and Garbles was the only Highland Heritage that was ever passed on to me. It takes only a trip to the isles to bring such atavistic notions upon you.

Mull is a wee island and very green as you come upon it by boat. We arrived, Colin of the blond moustaches already awash with whisky, and me trying hard to resist another dram of the Macallan, in Craignure. Craignure is very small indeed with a handful of houses, a small pub and hotel, a miniature railway, nearby Torosay Castle crenellated in the distance, and signs telling you that the seat of the MacLeans of Duart, the castle of Duart itself, is a short distance away. The guide books tell you that Lord and Lady McLean are almost never away from their home and suggest, clearly absurdly, that they would welcome you dropping in for the odd scone or two. There was another signpost. It pointed to the only town on the island, Tobermory. A quick squint at the barren landscape around you would tell you that while Tobermory was hardly likely to be Las Vegas, it was going to be a sight more habitable than the great stretches of bogland which we were standing in. There was a road of sorts.

Bogland this island mainly is. The single track road to Tobermory passes through land in which little could grow or live. This is desert, green, wet, alive with insects, but land in which few mammals could survive for long. It is also, as you look past the blue of the water and the purple of the hills and islands across from you, breathtaking. I experience an actual intake of breath itself, the way you do when you first see the Alpine peaks of Switzerland. Very like that too. Calenders for real. Robert Wilson singing 'Down In The Glen'. 'The Tangle O' The Isles'. For a minute I thought back to my childhood, and Wilson and MacKellar and Father Sydney McEwan, all the Scottish and Irish tenors. This was what the words, hitherto quite meaningless as well they would be to a boy brought up in the dusty city; this was what the words had been describing. Through Salen there was a fence covered in washing, drying in the sun. The Tangle O' The Isles meant a washing still had to be done.

It takes a time, even with Donald Campbell driving, to get to Tobermory and when you do the very first sight of it is delightful. What you have in front of you is oddly familiar, something to do with childhood. It suddenly occurred to me what it was. There used to be a big train-set at the Kelvin Hall when I was a kid. It was based on this. There lay the sea made out of mirror glass. The banks of the well-organised bottle green trees. The little harbour and the dolls houses bright and sharply painted. Tobermory is a toytown. It is clean and crisp and delightful to look at. But it is toytown all the same.

It turns out that it is, in way, exactly that. Tobermory was celebrating its 200th anniversary, for it is an invented town, created in 1788 by the fifth Duke of Argyle and the then British Fisheries Society. It is but a little bigger now, with new cottages up the hill from the waterfront, neat little domiciles, harled in the grand old tradition of the council house. There is only one concourse which is packed with delicate little houses painted, oddly, in primary colours. The Mishnish Hotel is an incongruous shocking pink. Later I have to investigate the interior of the bar, but there are other delights to be gone through first. A walk down the waterfront discovers bizarre little shops with names like Mix N' Match: boutiques for heaven's sake. There is a tourist centre which sells inaccurate maps and even more inaccurate, or at least perfunctory, guide books costing the earth. Halfway along a promenade is a gaily-painted well with a cast iron sculpture of a child adorning the top: a miniature version of the Copenhagen infant. A recent observer reported Tobermory to be booming with tourism and enterprising business. I saw a handful of elderly English Widows looking for somewhere so quiet as to be next door to Eternal life, and a small group of teenage French girls finding English money impossible. The Tobermory Distillery had closed down some time before.

Thinking that we could leave the delights of Tobermory night-life to, well, night, we decided upon a trip to other parts. There was a place called Dervaig on the map. We made for there. Dervaig is to the west and it doesn't take a genius to see that, like that other island not far away, Ireland, this land can hardly support human life. Yet like Donegal, it clearly did once, but God knows how. Passing a lone shell of a sheiling you have to think of how arduous a life it must have been here for the people, and it was. For centuries the Scots were the most poverty-stricken people in Europe. It could have been my own folk who lived and laboured, pointlessly, here. 'Someday, son all this could be yours... '. Not for the last time did I realise how wonderful even the slums of Glasgow must have looked to my Grandparents, away from this endless toil against the elements. Ludicrously, when we got to Dervaig, set in a low valley, there was a row of streetlights. Ludicrously for there was one street and perhaps ten houses. Even more bizarre was the shop.

It was a small, very ramshackle, two-roomed shop with a couple of little wooden tables on which we were served coffee and Club biscuits. Hanging from a rafter were strings of garlic and a Parma ham. Boxes of Brie lay beside packets of Arran oatcakes on a dresser. There were racks of books. I took a look at the titles. There was Gertrude Stein, and Doris Lessing, D.H. Lawrence, Raymond Chandler. In the middle of all this incongruity were a fine tortoiseshell cat and a lumbering chap in sweater and flannels. He was serving a number of English Tourists. You could tell they were English by their children. English children always have pink and white faces and washed out hair. The shopkeeper was English too. His name was Hugo Pitman and he had initially been a newspaperman who had come up here nineteen years ago to interview old Rab Butler and had then just stayed.

All over Mull I was to find recent immigrants, mostly from the south of England. Hugo – or David, as he preferred to be called – had come here, set up shop, and taken over the Mull Little Theatre. This establishment proved to be a small but pleasant sort of barn with 43 seats. It was mainly tourists who came – the current play was about Bonnie Prince Charlie and Flora McDonald – and few Scot locals bothered to go. Needless to say it was an uphill struggle to keep it afloat.

Back in Tobermory the rain which had been thin and desultory had become a downpour and the Mishnish bar looked inviting. This is owned by Mull's only celebrity, Bobby McLeod, ex-provost of Tobermory and leader of one of those accordion type bands which I loathe so much: he is to be heard regularly on Radio Scotland. Behind the bar were two very bonnie barmaids – the wet but mild climate of this part of the world produces complexions on the young girls which no amount of artifice from Estee Lauder could emulate – and thirty-six optics as well as a plethora of bottles behind them. A number of locals stood at the bar talking among themselves and largely ignoring the foreign yachtsmen. It was too wet for even the yachtsmen to go out and I listened, amazed, at the wild and clearly enhanced, tales of past voyages. You get the same from climbers and fishermen. Outside it grew dark and the mirror glass of the bay reflected the lights. It was so pretty it was hard to take it seriously. The bar began to full up with local youths. They sounded like Glaswegians for the Glasgow accent is now ubiquitous throughout much of Scotland. Curiously the older Mull Islanders possess little idiosyncrasy of speech that I could hear.

Later that night in the Western Isles Hotel where we were staying – it is the only decent hotel in Mull – they announced last orders at midnight. Residents were supposed to go into what I had seen already to be a very pleasant lounge but the door was locked. It was suggested that I could take my drink up to my bedroom if I liked. I said I wouldn't bother: it reminded me of 'THE LOST WEEKEND', and rather dispiritedly I went up to bed. The bar staff remained in the bar, sitting over their own drinks. I had a sudden curious remembrance of going to bed as a child, resentful of the adults who could stay up.

Next morning the breakfast was adequate as had been dinner the night before. Like most places in Scotland it was a little unimaginative though it was served in an extremely pretty dining room. The waitress had been very polite but a little distant. I looked out of the breakfast room window at the pale drizzle, across the bay and it's bobbing yachts, and thought where to go next. Colin on the ferry across had told me of a little pub: he said it is the smallest pub in Britain. In Pennyghael, to the south west of the island.

Actually it isn't the smallest pub in Britain: that honour belongs to a bar in Bury St. Edmunds where you can only squeeze in three customers. The Kinloch Bar is pretty small at that, though there is another bar butting on to it. Angus Brown and his wife Fiona own it. Angus worked for a brewery in Edinburgh for years and is another immigrant to Mull. His daughter is at Glasgow University. It is a nice enough wee place he has though he has refurbished it. My heart sinks every time I hear the word refurbished and I can't help but wonder what glorious wood panelling lies covered up throughout the length and breadth of Scotland. Another group of elderly tourists stroll in and order coffee though it is well after mid-day and a respectable enough hour to have a swift one. Are all elderly English tourists tee-total?

They probably are, the ones who come to Mull. People looking for quietness. Just as the immigrants have come for the quiet. These are people determined to get out, as they tell you copiously, 'of the rat race'. Mull's own booklet boasts of this: of its contrast with 'the pressures of modern city and urban life': of the 'highly skilled and qualified people doing things for which they are totally untrained but doing them, extremely well'.

For the truth is that, as in many places in Scotland, Mull is quiet almost to the point of stupor. That even the lack of effervescence which these English seekers after perfect peace bring with them cannot match the apathy of the majority of Mull islanders who remain, and so the English end up owning all the little craft shops and all the little businesses. That the young people with vigour leave as soon as they can – and mostly have to. That the English bring this camera of solitude with them and chase the young people with spirit away. Not, I suppose that they wouldn't have gone anyway, for there is little to support a real economy. Mull's beauty cannot sustain you all the year round, let alone for life. I got on the ferry across to Oban. It'll be down to Glasgow as soon as possible: it won't take long. I looked from the bows of the boat to see the green island. For a last look. As my grandparents must have done these long years ago. Never to return.

Auld Reekie

WHY EDINBURGH? And what was the young man in the Donegal tweed suit clutching an incongruous umbrella doing in that dirty hall all those years ago? The young man in the tweeds was I and it was matriculation day at Edinburgh College of Art.

143

Around me were other, rather younger, people (for I was what they called 'a mature student') and I must have cut a strange figure among them, for they were all heavily engaged in trying to look as much like art students as they could. They'd been practising all summer; doubtless much to the despair of their parents.

The boys had the obligatory long hair, jeans, open waistcoats. Those who could manage it sported scruffy little wisps of beard or a Crosby, Stills and Nash moustache. The girls had long Baez-style locks and white-painted faces with enough mascara on them to black a cavalry officer's boots. Skirts were so short they were simply a kind of pelvic bandage. I went back to Glasgow that night wondering what I had done to myself.

Why Edinburgh? It was a strange choice for a Glaswegian. There was only one other student from the magic city and she was a lassie. Edinburgh had been my first choice, actually. I suspect I was partly influenced by the recent film of The Prime of Miss Jean Brodie and could imagine myself as Robert Stevens seducing some delicious young schoolgirl in the art room. I imagined the city as especially pretty, too. Perhaps it was mere wanderlust – I had had a three year sojourn in London and had spent some time in Ireland before returning to native Glasgow. Now I was here in Edinburgh.

For some three weeks I commuted daily but the travelling took four hours a day. I moved into an appalling bedsit and immediately settled into college life. I began to find the other students less alien and forbidding (they were most of them, after all, seven or eight years younger than I.) From their view point I must have seemed some kind of link with authority and the real grown-ups. I'd even been teacher before going to the college.

Outsiders will find it hard to imagine life at an art college. For a start it is very intense. There are small numbers of students (Edinburgh, the largest art college in Scotland, has a first-year intake of just over 100), and everybody knows everybody. Even the quietest most demure, students gets known. Nobody can be lonely at an art college.

And the hours are so long. Where the Yooni students were strolling about with two lectures and a tutorial a week, the art students were working from nine to half-six all day, and later that would get much longer. Seven days a week at that. And there is a paradoxical authoritarianism at art college. Far from the public notion of an unfettered bohemian existence, the students had to answer a roll call in the morning and dodging off was greatly frowned upon.

Outright paternalism was rife. The students were not permitted a bar, I remember, despite the fact that their contemporaries up at university were falling down nightly in their union beer bar. This was a highly contentious issue in my day, and gave vent to enormous resentment. Oddly enough, the art students still don't have a bar as a five year experiment proved a failure a while back.

But there were other delights all the same. One of them was the lecturers themselves, a glorious eccentric bunch. The principal, Stanley Wright, wandered seemingly aimlessly round the college, clad in a suit of boldly checked plus-fours and a Glengarry bonnet. There was Kingsley Cook of the design department, who had invented a quite pointless art form consisting of tea trays filled with different coloured inks and oils. 'Here lies the body of Coogsley Kink, who died in a tray of his cosmic ink' ran a slogan in the college club gents. (Talking of graffiti here, there was a splendid *trompe-l'œil* urinal which a smart-assed student had painted on the lavatory wall, often confusing the inebriated students.)

Robin Philipson was head of the school and made wonderful appearances in the studios in the late afternoons, dressed magnificently in a superbly cut dark blue suit, the lapels of his waistcoat flowing a carnation in his buttonhole, and his suede winkle-pickers stepping out smartly as his distinguished leonine head graced the corridors.

David Michie, now head of drawing and painting at the college himself, would stroll up to your easel, take a squint at what was on it, twitch his beard, and utter loudly and cheerfully, 'Rubbish, my boy, absolutely rubbish,' and taking a battered packet of fags from his pocket would proffer it to you. 'Have an Embassy,' he would cry.

You could go on forever about the lecturers. I may say that their talents as artists were hotly disputed by the students nightly in Clark's Bar, for the apprentice is ever finer than his master. They were held in considerable awe all the same.

The art college is much changed these days. A brand new building has been added to the old one and is more hideous, too – which is quite a feat as the old art college is about as opposite as you could imagine to Glasgow's Rennie Mackintosh wonder. It is ugly, graceless, characterless, and shabby.

The fire station that lay at the entrance of the old college is still there, but is now a fire brigade museum, probably much to the chagrin of the firemen because they spent a great deal of their time ogling and chatting up the exotic female art students whom they fondly imagined, as most lay people do, to be boisterously promiscuous.

The work of the college is changing, too. There is an increasing commercial awareness in every department, for art colleges are now as much part of big business as university science and engineering facilities have become. It irritates the principal of Edinburgh Art College, John Paterson – whom I remember as a lecturer for first-year students – that the public, even at professional levels, continue to perceive the art college experience as something out of Henri Murger or George Du Maurier, operatic starving in arrests and folks in big floppy hats.

'Even the so-called fine artists among the students,' he told me, 'took in £15,000 at last year's degree show.'

Degree shows, now. I did a diploma and could see nothing wrong with being distinguished from those yooni chaps in such away. The qualification itself meant less to an artist than it did to other students because the vocation was essentially untied to monetary success and, I suspect, this is still largely the case.

Mind you, there are differences between the students of 20 years back and those of today. John Paterson himself admitted that art students, in common with students in other disciplines, are perhaps more serious than they were, and he rather regrets the passing of the 'fine madness' of yesteryear. While recognising that art colleges have had to be more aggressive in selling themselves to outsiders both in government and industry, he also feels the colleges should never lose the kind of individualism which was marked in the postwar years. David Michie agrees and I got the impression that the whole degree situation – the college now has degrees that link with both Edinburgh and Heriot-Watt Universities – is the least of his concerns. The art always comes first.

Certainly my investigations in the college recently appear to prove the notion that the students themselves are far less manic. Almost every area of the college has a no-smoking sign – this in a place where most students smoked assiduously, and it is by no means tobacco they were inhaling when I was a student. Many a budding artist then was blasting his head off with Afghan Black.

The corridors were strangely quiet. I remember six games of heavy football going on there. The dreary sculpture court, once enlivened by such outrages as classical statuary with the private parts liberally smeared with luminous paint so

147

that Augustine pricks could glow in the dark, is now the recipient of displays of town-planning diagrams. Many of the male students wear collars and ties.

True, many of the students looked much the same as we did – girls in thick black tights, boys in filthy paint-spattered jeans – but I could see little of the kind of wild excesses which my generation went in for. A quiet and, rather austere, scene it seemed. I went in search of the other splendours of being an art student in Edinburgh: the city itself.

Edinburgh is not Glasgow: it cannot be compared with it. It continues as different as Alden found it to be. 'Well set Edinburgh,' he called it in Nightmail; 'working Glasgow.' It shows, too. The remarkable rejuvenation of Scotland's biggest city has not been matched by its capital. Despite the possession of some of the most glorious Georgian architecture in the world, Edinburgh seems resigned to a douche dullness about such splendour.

The fine buildings are coated with black grime. Stone-cleaning and refurbishment is little in evidence. The famous Hole in the Ground which was intended many years back as an opera house is now an ugly modernistic shopping centre at the far end of Princes Street, which itself is populated by grubby frontages and incongruous new developments.

The famous Rose Street – scene of many a student pub crawl – now looks down at heel, pampered, and littered with broken glass, plastered by cheap fly-by-night shops. Such new ideas that exist are piecemeal and clearly not followed through by any sort of city plan. Edinburghers are indeed highly conscious of this, and of the stark contrast with their rival in the west, and put it down to the idiocies of their Labour run council. Few seem to realise that Edinburgh is the third largest financial centre in Europe.

The housing schemes outside the city would pass for Soweto and make Glasgow's problem estates like quiet suburbs. There is a fair amount of despair about and a marked lack of what Mrs Thatcher likes to call 'enterprise'.

Enterprise in Edinburgh is for the wealthy and the middle class who live in the city centre and the New Town. The Edinburgh working class is the most deferential, and the most depressed, of any city in Scotland. The middle class is the most smug and complacent.

Edinburgh is not as aggressive a city as Glasgow and that has its benefits, too. I asked two policemen the way to the famed Milne's Bar, haunt of MacDiarmid, and they could not have been friendlier and more cheerfully courteous. In Milne's Bar itself the barmen were surly and punters laughed at my hat. It would be exactly the opposite in Glasgow.

I visited a number of the watering holes which were student stamping grounds in my day. The Abbotsford's still closed down in the afternoons and this in a city with unimaginable levels of late-night opening. The Cafe Royale oyster bar was closed and the beautiful bar itself ruined by a ludicrously fake erection around the mahogany counter. I remember it was not so long ago that this wonderful building was nearly pulled down. Sandy Bell's – that famed folk emporium – rang to no guitar over lunchtime and I could see no students lecturing tutors like the scholarpoet Hamish Henderson, as occurred when I was an habitue.

A fine example of the kind of po-facedness of the city today is the objection by Mr Timothy Clifford, controversial director of the National Gallery, to the installation of a delightful nineteenth-century carousel outside his building. Not 30 yards away lies a hot-dog stand. Mr Clifford himself has created interiors in his gallery which would pass for Goldberg's at its most vulgar. For Edinburgh has become, in fact, another city than it was when I studied here those years ago and it is difficult to imagine how, or why, they have achieved that. Glasgow's ex-Lord Provost Michael

Kelly, has got his work cut out to make the place miles better believe me.

And yet, despite the fact that I never felt at home in Edinburgh, I spent five great years there. The substance of that is that during the five years I rarely went home. Back wandering around the art college – which has proved in the end to be somewhat inconsequential to me now that I earn my living by writing – I could feel a little of the great Caledonian anti-zyzygy which the two cities clearly represented in their way. And it still upset me that I could no longer get an Embassy out of my old lecturer, David Michie. He chucked the fags years back.

The Highlands

WHAT I WILL tell you is that I never did geography at school: it wasn't long ago that I discovered Stirling was north of Glasgow. I regard Eaglesham as the Highlands, for heaven's sake. And the first time I was sent to Fort William I nearly rang up relations in Canada to prepare them them for my visit. (I imagined a structure made out of pointed wooden stakes, with red-coated mounties prancing about). When I was at school only dunderheids did Geography; we intellectuals went in for history. And I knew the history of Glencoe.

Glencoe is the eerie place I once spent a night alone in a tent in and you can imagine the massacre even without a drink in you. You go through the place to get to the Great Glen, just as you go through Loch Lomondside, past the caravans and the B&B's and the hotels determined to catch you out in your peckishness with the promise of a spurious bar meal and a pint of good old traditional keg beer. This the scenery which has embedded itself in the Scottish psyche and which few really know – a few over keen climbers perhaps, maybe the inhabitants. For most it is quite simply a playground for a few days and its grandeur is mainly viewed through unremitting drizzle. But it is through this combination of epic splendour and barrenness which you go to get to the town of Fort William.

A nasty town, Fort William is, set in a landscape which even Frank Lloyd Wright could not have buggered up, but which his adherents have had a right good go at. Despite the presence of local stone the planners of Fort William fell in love with concrete and breezeblocks and tried their hardest to make the town look like Cumbernauld with mountains. Despite the appalling appearance of the place, the locals are grand people, as I have found out before, and was to re-discover on my visit.

But first things first. I was not here to hobnob with the average teuchter: I was here to see the top hotel in the land for myself. Inverlochy Castle. Trencheryob is never done talking about it. Derek Cooper, the English gourmet, is the boy for extolling its virtues. Foreign chaps are hardly away from the place when they can get a booking. Its fame has spread even to your Urban Voltaire and thus it was that it was myself turned up after my journey through the splendour of the West Highlands and found myself propelled into this most exclusive of hotels.

Inverlochy Castle is set among its own grounds of 500 acres and surrounded by landscaped gardens and rhododendrons and ... I got all that off its brochure. You can't fool me with that drivel. I was brought up in an area in practically the middle of the city which had about 500 acres of blitzed bomb site and rhododendrons are of very recent date to this country and came from the Himalayas. You should see the herb garden at Inverlochy Castle but. It is the size of Pollock Estate.

And inside the castle itself, inside the hotel, you feel as if you're acting in a movie. This is the Highland holiday on a grand scale. Queen Victoria spent a week here in 1873, (the brochure told me that too and I couldn't help pondering, doubtless irreverently, that it could have been in the same week that Rangers Football Club was founded. 'Your Majesty, the Teddy Bears have just kicked off ...' Well, it's possible, isn't it. John Brown was a prod after all, and instead of the Empress of India the joint now regularly caters for King Hussein, that most un-Arab of Arabs.)

Empresses of India or Kings of Jordan or not, it is certainly the place for nabobs and even Glasgwegian nabobs such as myself. The bedroom was bigger than my flat and the bathroom would have washed the entire features desk of this blatt in a one-er, if they had a mind to wash at all. Opening a wardrobe I discover that dressing gowns are provided. I have been in hotels where you have to provide your own disinfectant. There were two lavatories and I pledged myself to empty them both and make sure the facilities were suitably used up.

Nothing would do but a visit to the billiard room. I put up with Mr Galloway, the photographer and his insensate demand for poses at the billiard table, but only if he agreed to be soundly thrashed at snooker. The billiard room proved to be a compact little room with an especially old table and a collection of snooker cues which were bizarre in their inaccuracy. Curly cues, you might call them, and as good an excuse as myself and Jim the photog could come up with for taking an hour to pot four balls.

Around the room were the heads of luckless beasts which old Lord Abinger had felled in hunting expeditions. There were about eight big furry heads of mountain elks with antlers like trees on them which, according to the legend written underneath, had been shot by the noble lord in Jackson Lake, Wyoming. Abinger of bad fortune right enough.

There is also a library in the billiard room, and a wonderful collection of books with splendid titles like The Letters of Queen Victoria, or Central African Game and its Spoors; my favourite tome was King Edward VII as a

Sportsman. It is easy to see that old Lord Abinger was almost a Proustian intellectual. A sudden burst of egalitarianism came upon me. Why should this wonderful establishment have belonged to a bloke with an IQ of fifteen?

Down stairs for dinner, but first a few pre-prandials in the magnificent hall. Mr. Michael Leonard, the boss around here, (I have already met the owner, a fine-looking lady called Grete Hobbs: nothing is too good for the visitors here), and he proves to be a soft-spoken Irishman; Mr. Leonard does it right. At Inverlochy your whisky comes immediately but with such discretion you hardly realise you are being waited on hand and foot. Underneath the chandeliers and the frescoed ceiling amidst all the splendour of the place are more than myself.

Around the fireplace are a party of clearly well-heeled Americans. Not your brash sort at all. They remind one somehow of a family out of an Agatha Christie movie. I am almost right. It IS a family, the Cock's from New Orleans. Mr. Cock is a stockbroker it seems and he has come across with his grown-up family just for a few days, to celebrate his birthday. At dinner they are animated but civilised. At dinner I am agog at the wonder of the grub. The photographer is agog enought to eat enough for the entire Cock family and on his own.

When it comes to coffee in the hall it is dark outside and the sort of satisfied feeling you can only get after the best of grub steals over me: I get to feel that I DESERVE this. In a setting such as Inverlochy you can almost see Mrs Thatcher's point of view. The American family are all, as we say in Glasgow, well-relaxed, and towards eleven the paterfamilias rises and says goodnight, happily, and I am bound to state, a little tipsilly, he waves with dignity to us all as he descends the staircase to his suite. His wig is just a little askew. Oddly, it lends to his patrician air.

It is but a short time before I find myself engaged in discussion with two local worthies and their wives; (they recognised me in fact. There's fame for you). Joe and Alistair press a drink upon us and when I mention that I'd like a wee nocturnal trip around Fort William itself, a phone call is made, and a note tucked into my hand, for there is nothing open after midnight in Fort William due to the Sabbath. 'There is still a bit of the Wee Free stuff about', says Alastair MacGregor who turns out to be the owner of several nightclubs all over the Highlands, including the up-market Electric Whispers in Perth, as well as Gregory's disco in Fort William itself.

Gregory's is packed full of young teuchters having a good time the way young people anywhere have a good time – in the dark, hotter than a full-blast sauna, and with your ears dropping off with the noise. Downstairs was the only place for me because upstairs I suspected I was going to get thrown out for over-age drinking. Downstairs I meet Charlie Prosser and his chums who are only too happy to toss a few whiskies down my throat. A young blonde girl with beguiling eyes tells me my TV show was great. Mind you she also thought Andy Cameron was handsome. A couple of locals get put out for throwing chips at each other: in Glasgow they'd have been throwing glasses.

Later, when the young people have gone I find myself chatting away to a bloke I taught in Hamilton. Colin MacLean, he is, and soon to start on lunchtimes on Radio Clyde. I remember him from Radio Tay. A tall, slightly drunken youth invites us all to a party. Unlike the other spots I have visited on this soujourn, For William is packed with bright and happy welcoming people who are looking for fun. It is an ugly town but there is confidence here.

After a magnificent breakfast in Inverlochy the next morning, watching the Americans go off in clouds of expensive plaid suits and Hermes scarves, taking a last look at the gilded chairs, the superb paintings and object d'art –

there is nothing repro in Inverlochy – bracing myself to return to Glasgow, we decide to take a squint at other local spots. A wee drift up the Caledonian Canal and a look at our biggest mountain, Ben Nevis, is in order.

They kept on about this Caledonian Canal when I was a kid. They way I heard it I thought it was like Panama. In reality it is practically a burn. It is hard to see how it could have cost nearly one and a half million quid back in 1822, but a lot harder to see why it was made in the first place. As schoolboys knew in my day it didn't work out anyway and is now largely used by Hooray Henries in their yachts. 'Yaffa Yatt? Whit yatt ye affa?' as the noble Bud once said. Neptune's staircase is a series of locks which will take you a day to get through and bloody boring it must be too but there are lots of waterproofed mariners about.

A fat English girl in an orange suit shouting across at a chinless fellow in what looks like a school janitor's cap. 'I say, Rodney,' she exclaims. It is so archetypical I suspect a put-on but the school jannie turns around and cries 'What, old thing?' and I realise that the English cling to real-life cliches. I note one of the byelaws of the canal threatens a fine of forty shillings for anybody using 'scurrilous, abusive, offensive, or threatening language on or near the canal,' and shut my mouth instantly. The size of the yachts suggest that the owners could BUY Inverlochy Castle let alone spend a night there. Time, I thought, for a photo of Ben Nevis.

We travelled up and down that bloody road looking for Ben Nevis. We knew it must be near because there were droves of elderly English lades in white perms dragging their old retired menfolk with them. I ask one of the ladies the way to the legendary peak. For some reason she thinks I intend to go up it, dressed as I was in a pearl-grey suit and a fedora. We never found the biggest mountain in Britain. Shrouded in mist no doubt. The tourists were taking snaps of a big sonsie kiltie who proved to be German and bought snake-meat burgers from van painted tartan.

It was late when we got to Glasgow, and dark. An orange lamp burned in the window of my little South-Side club. Inside I knew there would be noise and banter and a glass of the amber fluid awaiting. Scotland suddenly seemed a long way off with its glens and rivers and disappearing mountain peaks. Another country it is from where I live, though so many of us once came from those places. It was good to be home, I thought and swung open the doors of Heraghty's.

The Way We Were

MY FATHER was born in the Gorbals, of Highland parentage, and that was my first Glasgow though I don't remember anything of that time in the classic (and somewhat mythical) slum: I was very wee when we moved from the district to a prefab in the douce little village/suburb of Cathcart. Up the road were the big houses with the bourgeoisie in them, but the local primary school was for everybody and Glasgow is basically democratic anyway. The result was that my early years were spent in a sort of middle-class environment without the money.

That mattered little anyway because the immediate post-war years were a great leveller financially. There were green trees and grass: Linn Park was a minute away. I remember my mother walking through the woods there, picking up pine cones and acorns for us little ones. The big houses had striped sunblinds on their porches. We were building a new world.

It changed, as it would, suddenly. My father's job, as a school janitor, took us away from that sunlit idyll. I might not have noticed the change too greatly: I say I might not, if it hadn't been for the miasma of tragedy which overhung this event for both my parents. My mother had been brought up in a middle-class family and even yet her mother and brothers owned bought houses far away in rural Ayrshire. My father had struggled for 20 years to escape the Glasgow slums. Yet both of them, with their progeny, were back in the most stygian of Glasgow's – and Europe's – slums: Townhead.

If my first sight of Glasgow had been uncharacteristic with its greenery and semi-agricultural suburban prospects, my second sight of it was all that Glasgow was meant to be in the popular imagination of the day. Townhead was dark and insanitary enough to pass for the most lurid illustrations of a mid-Victorian novel. I took solace in mid-Victorian novels which my grandma issued to me – books like Silas K Hocking's Her Benny (an especially popular novel of 1850's), in which, by dint of luck, Dickensian coincidence, and a moral rectitude which would have done credit to Little-by-Little Eric, the barefoot and ragged child protagonist emerged in manhood as a sterling chap falling heir to an estate, wealth and an upper-class bint well worth a dent, as they say. I fell for it.

But Townhead was entirely a Victorian novelist experience for me: like Dicken's blacking factory, like Dickens, it has never left me. The sheer *gloom* of the place and it's institutions. The back courts with their evil-smellng washhouses and middens and air-raid shelters. The poverty of the other children.

The girls had squints and unwashed hair dresses too thin for winter, skins pallid and smeared with impetigo and gentian violet. The boys were beefy and bullying or skinny and tubercular. Polio was rife. A boy called Abie who sat, reeking of sweat and urine, next to me in class, died of diphtheria: a girl whose only characteristic was the possession of haggard and grubby ringlets died in hospital of scarlet fever.

They gave you milk at playtime and they thought the world had changed. You were never done hearing about the refugee children in Europe and the displaced persons. In Townhead the entire population wasn't a kick in the arse off them.

In all those years my parents regularly packed us off to the South Side, to the George Cinema and the Kingsway (now a Freedom Hall for some unlikely Christian sect), on Saturday afternoons, where we watched Robert Taylor and Burt Lancaster and Jane Russell, and we went back through the half-remembered gardens of pleasant Cathcart and Mount Florida until it got dark and was time to take 104 bus back to the workhouses of Townhead.

In Townhead there were other children like me: the Duke's children, somehow sent, irrationally almost, to live with a peasant family, till the Duke decided we were ready. There were boys and girls in the very epicentres of these slum dwellings of the late forties and early fifties who were sent to dancing and piano and elocution lessons.

The blacking factory ended eventually. When I was 15 my father landed a school not far from the old Cathcart of 10 years before: in Merrylee, a housing scheme of such a celebration of decency that it would have satisfied a Jane Austin heroine. Naturally, I never really fitted in, though my younger brother did. It was, all the same, good to be back.

I have lived and worked in many cities and I have been back to Glasgow on three separate occasions, each one of which has brought more satisfaction than the last. Now, I have been back in the City of Culture for more than 12 years and it would take a hundred grand, an apartment in Manhattan, and a slightly younger Bo Derek than the present Bo Derek, to shift me. I live, still on the South Side, in a magnificent tenement flat of considerable splendour. I know the pubs, clubs, restaurants, shops and every bad-hat and vagabond worth talking to in this city, and feel like some kind of O. Henry in it.

Like every Glaswegian who learned his Glasgow on the streets, I sometimes feel I have more friends than I can cope with. I know I have to beware of smugness here: sometimes I have to beware of friends. This is *my* Glasgow: probably not much different, in fact, from yours. But mine all the same. I am glad to be here, to have been brought up in this. It is a good time now to be a Glaswegian for me, and for most of us too. It was not always so, and remember that.